The Amazing Adventures Of

The Teenage Alien

Best wishes
Sam Bryhar

SAM BRYHAR

Illustrations by David Haynes

The Amazing Adventures of DREF

Printed and bound in Great Britain by Sarsen Press, Winchester

A catalogue record for this book is available from the British Library

ISBN: 978-1-916722-12-5

ACKNOWLEDGEMENTS

Tony at Sarsen Press for his expertise and patience. Rebecca Dann for her copy-editing skills at such short notice. David Haynes (Wurz) for breathing life into the characters with his illustrations. Jack and Ella for their enthusiasm, encouragement, and critique. Kim for showing me the errors that I missed. Michelle Magorian for taking the time to look at the first draft at the Writers Conference and giving sound advice. A posthumous thank you to the late great and inspirational Leslie Thomas for his early comments and encouragement. Lastly but not least, a heartfelt thanks to the amazing Simon Squibb, whose generosity and entrepreneurship enabled DREF to become a reality.

DREF

by
Sam Bryhar

CHAPTER 1

5th June 1951

I was sliding headfirst down this dark slimy tunnel; something was caught around my neck, and I was being strangled. Intermittently, I was being squeezed; I could hear groaning and then a blinding light and suddenly everything stopped. The thing around my neck was being loosened. I wanted to breathe! Something had hold of my foot and suddenly I was upside down being hit around my backside. I started crying. As I opened my eyes, I saw a bunch of other eyes staring at me. I realised I was naked and covered in blood and slime.

Fourteen years later

We decided to cycle back along the footpath across the fields to get home before it was discovered that we were missing. Taking this route also reduced the risk of being spotted by Grumpy Grundon, the village policeman touring the beat in his van. At 4.30 in the morning, we couldn't say that we were just out for a ride! Unfortunately, I slid off the path into a plough furrow, which resulted in my chain flying off. I told the others to carry on and I'd probably catch them up before they got back. After a few minutes I was able to start on my way again. I had only cycled a few hundred yards when I became aware of a strange noise, which I can only describe as being like that of a short-wave radio that is not tuned in properly. The noise became louder and started pulsating in my eardrums. I looked up at the sky, half expecting to see one of the satellites that we had heard so much about recently, but instead what I saw was the most fantastic sight I had ever seen in my life! The noise became even more intense, so I let go of my handlebars and put my hands over my ears. At the same time, my front wheel became lodged in a rut and the next thing I knew I was entangled in a barbed wire fence, my shirt was ripped, and I could feel warm blood dripping down my arm. I quickly gathered my senses and tried to focus my eyes back to where I had seen the 'object' in the sky.

The noise was by now diminishing and the 'object' was moving away. As it did so I was able to make out a shape which looked like one of the giant ocean-going liners that I had seen all lit up at night in the Southampton Docks, but it was much more rounded and streamlined, almost cigar shaped. As the craft glided off towards the rising sun, my head felt decidedly like a plate of scrambled eggs - a mixture of excitement, fear, and apprehension - had I really fallen asleep whilst riding my bike and just merely dreamt it? Whatever, I decided there and then that I sure as hell was not going to tell anybody, for fear of being ridiculed! So, how was I going to explain the deep gash on my right forearm? Easy - I was always falling off my bike whilst performing wheelies and such like, and this would be just another one of those mishaps!

However, not even in my wildest dreams - or nightmares - could I have imagined what was about to confront me as I rounded the next clump of bushes as I crossed into Verdons Paddock. There standing right in my path was this enormous creature that was about five feet long and looked like a cross between an alligator and a prehistoric lizard. I felt the hair stand up on the back of my neck and right across the top of my head; I slammed on my brakes and once again nearly went over the handlebars. In a split second I visualised myself being catapulted straight into the jaws of this gruesome creature, then simultaneously my self defence mechanism tripped in, and I decided that the best plan of action was to throw my bike at the creature and run to the nearest tree as fast as my legs would take me and climb to the top before it ate me for breakfast! I was just about to put the survival plan into action when the creature reared up on its hind legs. Oh my god. This is it. I could feel the sweat starting to drip off my forehead, yet I was freezing cold, frozen in fact to the spot where I was standing. Suddenly, the creature started to

change shape, and after what seemed like an eternity but in fact was only seconds, the transformation was complete. I found myself now looking not at a prehistoric monster but a boy roughly the same age as me, dressed in what appeared to be a silver-coloured tracksuit. Before I could once again gather my thoughts, he said in a friendly voice:
"Hi, my name is Dref!"

I was totally flabbergasted! Was all this really happening to me or was I in bed asleep and in the middle of a most incredible dream? I touched my arm, which was still oozing blood as a result of being entangled in the fence, and it was very sore. Yes, this was real alright.

"Hello, I'm Andy," I replied, wondering if I was doing the right thing. I thought for a moment that perhaps I should just take to my heels and run, but then if this thing had just changed from a giant lizard into what appeared to be a boy not much older than me, there was no telling what he might be able to turn me into.

"Pleased to meet you," he said holding out his hand again in a friendly manner.

I shook it warily … but he felt normal enough. "How the devil did you do that?" I asked.

He looked at me, puzzled, for a moment. "Oh, that," he said. "We do that all the time where I come from; we call it formalizing. When we come down from our base station onto a different planet, we change ourselves into whatever life form the creatures are in the immediate vicinity. By doing that, we don't appear to be hostile. But you see I am a novice; in other words, I am only just learning and unfortunately, I forgot to activate my formalizer until a few seconds after I saw you, so I was still in the life form of the creatures I saw yesterday when I landed in the jungle on the other side of your planet."

"So where do you come from?" I asked.

"I come from the planet 'Mondern', which was in a far-off galaxy but unfortunately our planet became uninhabitable due to toxic pollution," Dref explained, with a ring of sadness in his voice. I was becoming more and more fascinated by what I was hearing. It was as if I was talking to a character who had stepped straight out of the 'Dan Dare' comic strip! I was no longer frightened, but I was becoming more and more curious by the second. The strange encounters that I had experienced in the last half hour were now starting to be explained and the object I had seen in the sky was obviously the base station where Dref came from.

Whilst I wanted to stay and learn more about this curious being, I was becoming very much aware that it was now daylight and John and Mike would be wondering what had happened to me and on top of that, Dad would soon be up and about feeding the chickens and if he found out that I wasn't there I would be definitely in for the high jump! "Look Dref, I am really sorry, but I am afraid I have got to go. I am not even supposed to be here but why don't we meet up again this afternoon, say at about three o'clock?"

Dref looked at the sun which had just come up on the horizon and said, "That's in ten hours' time." I looked at my watch, it had just turned five o'clock. "Yes, that's right." Poor chap, I thought! Obviously, his watch has stopped working; he must tell the time by the sun!

I said goodbye and made my way home. When I got back to the front gate, I could hear a rustling coming from behind the hedge. Oh no, not more surprises? Then, all of a sudden, Mike leapt out in front of me.

"Where have you been?" he asked in a hushed voice. "We were worried sick about you."

Wouldn't you like to know! I thought. But even if I told him what had happened, he would not have believed me, so I told him that my chain came off again and I ended up wrapped around the barbed wire fence alongside old Mother Yates's back garden and showed him the gash on my arm to prove it. He just gave me a sly smile as if to say, 'you clumsy clot', and beckoned me with a twitch of the head towards the tent. I leaned my bike up against the apple tree, crawled in through the flap and slid into my sleeping bag. John was already sound asleep and twitching just like old Bruce my dog! I put my head on the pile of clothes that I was using as a makeshift pillow and tried to go to sleep, but each time I closed my eyes all I could see were bright lights and overgrown lizards. I was just starting to doze off when John had one of his mega twitches and kicked Mike in the leg, who in turn shouted Ugh! which made me jump out of my skin - once again.

"You boys awake already?" I heard Dad ask. I just grumbled in response and turned over. What a hard day's night that was, I thought!

CHAPTER 2

The next thing I remember was a drowning sensation. I thought I had fallen in the brook that runs alongside the footpath. I opened my eyes only to find my dog licking my face, and John and Mike sat up in their sleeping bags laughing like hyenas. "Come on, Andy, you lazy toad. Time to get up! Can't you smell the bacon and eggs that your Dad's cooking for us? If you don't hurry up, we'll beat you to it and eat yours as well. Last one to the kitchen goes hungry!"

With that, we all leapt out of our sleeping bags, pulled on our jeans and raced down the garden. Following in hot pursuit was the dog barking like mad as if to threaten us not to eat his breakfast as well. We all dived through the kitchen door at the same time, and it swung open and hit the wall with such force I thought all the glass was going to drop out of it.

"Steady, steady!" my Dad boomed at the top of his voice, but like Bruce the dog, his bark was worse than his bite and sure enough our eyes were greeted with the sight of three delicious, cooked breakfasts on the table, waiting to be devoured by the 'Three Musketeers'. After we finished eating, it was time for John and Mike to go home, as they were going out sailing for the afternoon with Mike's parents. They had asked me if I wanted to join them, but I said no, firstly because if the sea was to get rough, I would certainly be seasick, and secondly, I had arranged to meet Dref in the afternoon and I was dying to find out what he was really all about!

The next few hours seemed to really drag but at last it was nearly time, so I told my mother that I was going to take the dog for a long walk, and off we went towards Aylings Meadow, which was where I had agreed to meet Dref. Bruce had run on ahead, and as I went through the gap in the hedge on the edge of the meadow, I could hear a lot of barking and I immediately thought that Bruce had met up with the farmer's dog, which strongly objected to anyone who ever passed close to his territory! However, when I could see clearly across the meadow, it appeared that Bruce had Dref cornered by the stile on the opposite side of the field. I whistled for him to come back to me and much to my surprise he did. He had a habit of acting deaf when he was enjoying himself being macho! I ran up to the stile where Dref was standing, but I noticed he did not look as bright and cheerful as he did when I left him ten hours ago.

"Hi, what have you been up to all day?" I asked.

"I've been waiting here for you to return, of course!" Dref replied. He spent the next hour and a half telling me all about himself. "Andy," he said in a very formal voice. "What I am about to tell you must not be repeated to anyone without my permission. It must be TOP SECRET, because if the wrong people find out who I am and where I come from, it could put me in great danger! As I told you earlier, I used to live on the planet Mondern until it was virtually destroyed by pollution. It was a truly beautiful place, and as yet I haven't seen anywhere on your planet Earth that compares with it, but we believe that there is such a place, which is why we are here. That is our mission: to find a suitable place for the inhabitants of our Mothership, Galled, to settle and make a new home. You see, we had warnings that the pollution and toxic waste was going to eventually make our planet uninhabitable, but by the time the authorities started to take notice it was too late, and thousands of people started dying so eventually we had to evacuate as much of the population as possible onto our twelve giant Motherships. They are all like the one you saw last night. The others are touring different galaxies looking for a suitable host planet just like we are. Although our planet was relatively small compared with planet Earth and we only had a population of about five million, the technology that we possess is far in advance of anything we have found so far on any other planet; the nearest we can find is here. You are no doubt wondering how I managed to change from a creature of the jungle into a humanoid like yourself? Well, when we are infants, we undergo a small surgical operation to have an electrical enhancer implanted in our bodies. It sounds gruesome but it's all quite painless really. It is like a pacemaker that some of your people have fitted to assist their heartbeat. In our case, this advanced technology has two superb uses; firstly, it enables our brains to transmit our voices in any language of man or beast, and secondly, it activates our formalizer, together with a beam sent from our base station which enables us to change into the creature in whatever surrounding we land in. I hope I'm not boring you, am I, Andy?"

"No, of course not, Dref. In fact, I'm lost for words … absolutely flabbergasted in fact!"

"You see, Andy, all this technology worked perfectly when we were living and operating from our planet Mondern, but now that we have been away for so long, our systems are running out of the vital energies needed to operate them. Consequently, some of our systems are starting to fail. For instance, this morning I was unable to activate my formalizer to beam me back to my base station, so I had to wait here all day for you to return, and I do not know when I can rendezvous again. In fact, I am a bit worried because as things are at the moment I'm stranded here!"

"Is there anything I can do to help?" I asked.

Dref thought carefully for a moment. "That is very kind of you, Andy, but if you're going to help, you must promise not to reveal my true identity to anyone, because if you do, it will mean great danger. In the history of our people, this has happened when we have landed on other planets, and we ended up being hunted like animals. It was terrible, and that is why our learned elders developed the formalizer."

"I understand; I think first we should see about getting you some food - you must be starving if you've been stuck here all day and haven't eaten. How about if you come to my house? I'll tell my Mum that you are one of my school friends and ask her if you can stay to tea. I'm sure it will be alright."

Dref looked a bit uneasy. "I only have three tablets a day; each one contains all the nutrients that we need to sustain our healthy bodies, but we did eat dehydrated food when we were at home. I don't know if I would be able to digest your type of food!"
Oh no! I thought, if there is one thing my Mum can't stand, it's a faddy eater. She likes people to clear everything that's put in

front of them. “Well, let’s give it a try, Dref. I think we’ll just have to take things one step at a time. C’mon, let’s go.”

CHAPTER 3

As we made our way back to the house my thoughts were racing like a record being played at the wrong speed. How would I explain his strange silver coloured tracksuit? Maybe I could lend him a pair of jeans and a t-shirt? What if he re-established contact with his mothership while we were having tea, and he suddenly did a disappearing act? What if - what if!!! Maybe I should practice what I had just preached to Dref and take one step at a time!

"I think we shall have to tell my parents that you are a school friend of mine, and you were out sailing with your mother and father and they had a problem with the boat, left you here at Hambridge while they've gone to get the repairs done, and you bumped into me down at the quay! Yes, I think it sounds reasonable. It's all a lie, and I don't like lying to my Mum and Dad, but I certainly can't tell them the truth, so that'll have to do for the moment. Can you remember that all right, Dref?" He nodded his head in approval but was looking more and more apprehensive the nearer we got to home. I attempted to reassure him. "I think you'll get on fine with my folks, Dref. They are really nice people and we've got some French students staying with us as well, and they're okay. When we get home in a minute, I'll tell Mother that you've got your sailing suit on and need a change of clothes. You're about the same size as me, so I should have plenty of things that will fit you."

The thought of putting on "humanoid" clothes and being able to blend in seemed to please Dref somewhat, and he relaxed a bit. As we approached the front gate, the dog was straining at the lead - he could obviously smell the dinner cooking! I let him off so that he could run on ahead to the back door. Dad and Mum were both in the kitchen preparing tea and looked a little surprised to see me standing there with a new companion. Before they had time to say anything, I announced that there would be another mouth to feed and assumed that it would be okay, which of course it was! I then made the introductions and told them the story - as we had agreed - of who Dref was and how he came to be with me. So far so good!

"C'mon then, Dref, let's go and get changed." As we were walking through from the kitchen into the hallway, unfortunately I forgot to tell Dref to give the dog, who was sat on his bed gnawing at a bone, a wide berth. Bruce growled and snapped and bared his teeth. At the same time his hackles went up all down his back, and for a moment he resembled a porcupine. To my absolute amazement, Dref growled and barked back, which took the dog so much by surprise he leapt off his bed and went and hid under the kitchen table with his tail between his legs.

“Nobody has ever thought of doing that to him before. I shall have to remember that it seems to be very effective,” said Dad with a chuckle.

When we got upstairs, I said to Dref, “I shouldn’t do that too often if I were you, or people will soon start thinking that you are strange, and before you know it, your cover will be blown! What on earth did you say anyway?”

“I told him that he could pack that in, or I would pick up the cow’s leg he was eating and hit him over the head with it. I didn’t mean to do it. The problem is caused by this faulty formalizer, and I can’t override it. It’s programmed to sense danger, humanoid or animal. It was what I think you call a reflex action.”

“Never mind, it was quite funny really. Here, try these jeans and t-shirt on, they should fit you.” As he peeled off his tracksuit, I couldn’t help noticing that he had an unusual amount of body hair, and just a single nipple in the centre of his chest!

He must have noticed me staring at him and remarked, “I’m not quite the same as you, am I, Andy?”

Within a few minutes Mother was calling us for dinner. Dref didn’t hear her at first; he was too busy looking at himself in the mirror and trying to get his thick black mop of hair to go into a quiff at the same time as looking back and forth from the mirror to the picture of Elvis Presley that was on my wall. I gave him a gentle poke. “C’mon, Mr. Vanity, you look very handsome, but all that will change if we don’t hurry up and get downstairs. Mother’s calling us for dinner.” He looked at me blankly, as if I was talking double Dutch, but duly followed me out of the bedroom and onto the landing where we promptly bumped into Michelle and Eva, the two French girls, coming out of their room across the way.

They looked quite astounded, casting their eyes on the new face in the house, and they obviously felt a bit awkward, if not bemused! I did the necessary introductions, during which Mother again bellowed up the stairs, so I beckoned to them all that we were now dicing with death!! So, I suggested that we chatted over dinner, and if we did not go down NOW, there wouldn’t be any dinner! As we sat down at the table for tea, Eva and Michelle were giggling and whispering between themselves, no doubt discussing the new arrival. Suddenly Dref started talking to them in fluent French. Their faces were an absolute picture, with mouths dropped open and cheeks turning crimson red. From the gist of the conversation, I managed to interpret that the girls had started to discuss Dref's anatomy, and to their astonishment he innocently asked them what their bodies were like! I could have died on the spot!

Mother was impressed by his fluent French, but not by the content of his answer; I could tell that by the classic 'I am not really amused' frown on her face! However, she was even less amused when Dref started eating his food with his fingers, but even though he felt the power of her steely glare, he must have suddenly realised that we had different table manners here than the natives he first encountered when he landed in the jungle! Either that or his formalizer was starting to play up again. Oh god, I hope he's not going to suddenly turn back into that giant lizard while we are all sat at the table, I thought to myself. My mind was racing, and I started jabbering about anything and everything just to try and keep Dref concentrated on our environment.

Finally, Dref picked up his knife and fork and said, "Pardonne-moi" and started eating normally. I couldn't help noticing Dad looking at Dref from under his glasses, and then glance back at me as if to say, 'you've brought a right one home this time son!'

The rest of the mealtime passed without further incident, thankfully. We all left the table; the girls scuttled off to their room, whispering as usual but with a hint of excitement in their voices, and Dref followed me out into the garden where I was going to feed the chickens. 'So how come you can speak French so well then?' I asked, rather peeved because he could obviously speak it far better than me!

"I told you!" he replied rather indignantly. "I can change into any creature and converse in any tongue, according to my surroundings, but the energy used in doing so has almost drained my formaliser completely. I must find some way of putting power back into it, or soon I shall lose all co-ordination and, worse still, I shall not be able to pick up the signal sent out from my base station when it's back in range. You've got to help me, Andy!"

There was an awkward silence, and I racked my brain as to how I could help Dref and save him from becoming what would amount to an out of control alien. I suddenly remembered that Dad had an old battery charger in his tool shed. "I wonder if that could be adapted to get the necessary charge from the mains?" I thought out loud.

"What's that you said?" asked Dref. I explained to him what I had just thought about, threw the rest of the corn to the chickens and we set off down to the shed so that I could show Dref what I meant, because he didn't really understand what I was talking about.

It took us about ten minutes to find the old charger. In Dad's shed everything has its rightful place. He knows where everything is but nobody else does! We pulled the old charger out from underneath the bench; it was covered in dust and grease and had the remains of a mouse nest hanging out of the back of it. Dref looked at it most inquisitively and carefully dusted it off, handling it almost as if he were a bomb disposal expert with an unexploded bomb! He was paying special attention to the ammeter and the connections. He then lifted the side of his shirt and just above his hips, he had what looked to me like two oversized moles side by side, then to my utter amazement he peeled them back as if they were stuck on with Velcro only to reveal further what looked like two electrical terminals.

He glanced at me a bit smugly half expecting me to show my astonishment at the fact he had just revealed to me more alien features. Surprised yet again as I was, I decided to play it cool! "Your people think of everything, don't they? After your final trick, nothing surprises me anymore." I replied, quite matter of factly.

Ignoring my comments, Dref said, "I think we can adapt the terminals to fit but I'm not sure we shall be able to get enough power out of this old gadget!" Sure enough, within a few minutes he succeeded in making a good contact, the old charger buzzed and crackled into life, and the ammeter showed that there was indeed a current flowing into his formalizer.

Dref beamed broadly from ear to ear, looking almost as if he'd been asleep with a coat hanger in his mouth! Within seconds, my ear drums were being pierced by a high-pitched screech. I tried to ask Dref what was happening, but nothing came out. I glanced at him and saw that he was turning both blue and transparent. I tried to disconnect the leads from his formalizer, but then I too started to turn transparent blue, and the high-pitched screeching increased even more until everything around was bathed in the blue glow. Suddenly, it went black, and the floor of the shed seemed to disappear, and it was as if we were falling into the bowels of the earth, down and down until we came to an abrupt and sickening stop. I must have blacked out.

CHAPTER 4

23rd October 1707

As I started to come round, I could feel rain falling on my face; I ran my tongue across my lips and tasted salt. I opened my eyes to find that we were laying on a rocky beach; the waves were thundering down onto the rocks, and the sea was mountainous. Out of the corner of my eye I could see Dref laying a few yards along the beach, just starting to stir. I scrambled towards him. "Dref, wake up! Where are we? What happened?"

"I missed the beam to the base station, and because you were standing so close to me, Andy, you became engulfed in the force field, and dragged along with me. When a beam is missed, we go into a time-warp, sometimes into the future, and occasionally back in time." As he was talking, he fiddled with the face of his watch, and it clicked open to reveal what appeared to be another inner face. Meanwhile, all around us there were large quantities of broken and splintered wood, and even more coming in on the breakers. I looked towards the horizon through the mist and rain, and I could just make out the shape of an old sailing ship with a broken mast and sails in tatters, leaning at a precarious angle against some rocks.

"Andy, according to my time locator we have landed in the year 1707!"

I was hoping that, at any second, I would wake up and discover that this was just another of my vivid dreams, but somehow I knew that wasn't going to happen. This was for real. "Okay, Dref, now we know which year we are in, how the heck do we find out exactly where we are, and furthermore how do we get out of this mess and back to our time?" Before Dref was able to reply, a gigantic wave came crashing down over the top of us and carried with it the body of a young sailor. Dref jumped up and stood back aghast. I immediately rolled the poor soul over onto his back and began pumping his chest as I had learnt to do at my first aid course, in the hope there was a remote chance that there was still a flicker of life left in him. For several minutes, I worked on him, but there was no response, and his face was blue. I turned to Dref and said, "It's no use, he's a goner. Give me a hand to drag him further up the beach and we'll cover him up." As we started to move him, his stomach heaved and what appeared to be about a gallon of water and seaweed gushed out of his mouth. I pumped his chest a few more times, and he started breathing short, sharp breaths.

"Hey Andy, where did you learn that from? You've brought him back from the dead. We need a booster to do things like that!" exclaimed Dref.

I ignored his patronising comment and suggested that he helped me make our patient, who was starting to regain consciousness, a little more comfortable by getting him up onto the grass. We sat him up, and he started mumbling deliriously, "The Admiral…tried to save the Admiral…think he got away in a boat."
"Admiral who?" I asked.

"Shovell, Cloudesly Shovell." Then he lost consciousness again.

But that was all he needed to say for me to work out where we were. I remembered from my history lessons at school that England's worst naval disaster occurred in October 1707 when Admiral Sir Cloudesly Shovell and four of his ships ran onto rocks off the Scilly Isles, and over 1,670 men lost their lives. So, that was where we had landed: right in the middle of a major maritime disaster. I explained this to Dref, who found it hard to comprehend. We decided that although we could do nothing that would change the course of history, we had no alternative but to help the victims, and rescue them wherever possible, before we could even think about reaching civilisation and formulating a plan that would enable us to get back into our time.

Between us, we managed to pull the young sailor further up the sandy beach, out of harm's way. The sea was still mountainous, and one of the enormous waves breaking could easily have dragged him back in again. By now he was breathing more normally, yet still not fully conscious. I pulled up some clods of grass and laid them on top of the sand I had scooped up as a makeshift pillow to try and make him as comfortable as possible.

Bobbing up and down between the waves, I spotted a rowing boat. I nudged Dref and pointed towards the boat, then beckoned him to follow me down the beach. When we were out of earshot, I suggested that we could swim out towards the boat, firstly to see if there was anyone in it, and secondly, we could use it to try and reach civilisation. On the horizon several other islands could now be seen. "What is 'swim'?" enquired Dref.

"Moving through the water like this." Almost mockingly, I wheeled my arms round in the motion of front crawl, as we walked into the water.

"Ah, you mean like a fish!" Dref exclaimed. Before I could utter another word, he formalized into a dolphin, just like he had turned from a giant lizard into human that first day I met him. It took me four or five minutes of strong swimming to reach the boat. Dref obviously reached it within seconds, and I could see his dorsal fin popping out of the water as he circled it, lifting his head out of the water and squawking every few seconds, showing off as usual.

There did not appear to be anyone in the boat; I grabbed hold of the side, and pulled myself in. To my astonishment, as I did so, I came face to face with another scruffy young sailor. He looked more dead than alive. Nevertheless, I could not prevent myself from falling on top of him, as Dref nudged me up the backside with his enormous nose, to help me into the boat. I struggled to untangle myself, but not before the 'corpse' sprang to life, drew a sword from his scabbard, and almost slit my throat in one swift movement. Then there was a whoosh of water, and the next thing I saw was Dref - in dolphin mode - flying through the air, slamming straight into the head of my assailant and landing back in the water on the other side of the boat! I seized the opportunity to jump on top of the cutthroat merchant who by now was lying half dazed and moaning in the bottom of the boat. I picked up his sword, and held it to his throat, not wanting to take any chances.

He opened his eyes, and they were full of terror. Momentarily he struggled, but as the blade touched the skin of his throat, he froze. "It's okay, I'm here to help. I don't want anything from you, neither will I harm you. Just calm down." My words of reassurance seemed to work, and I could feel his body relaxing and the tension easing from his muscles.

"Who are you?" he croaked in an Irish accent. "And what's with that idjut fish?"

Dref was still cavorting around the boat and periodically leaping out of the water to check everything was alright. "Oh, don't worry about him, he's a friend of mine, but if you get stroppy again, he'll have you, a bit like having a faithful dog really!" My head was now working overtime, and I was having to think on my feet. "I'm Andy, we came from one of the islands to try and help, but our boat got smashed on the rocks too. So, who are you?"

"Samuel Murphy, from Ballymena. I was a powder monkey on The Association."

He started telling me about his job on The Association, on which he'd served for nearly three years, and when he said that he had been taken on the day of his eleventh birthday, I realised that he wasn't even fourteen years old. Yet, with his shock of jet-black hair and wind beaten rusty complexion, he looked more like he was in his early twenties.

As he was talking, the wind shifted round to the east and was becoming stronger by the second and with no oars the boat was being thrown around like a cork. Suddenly, Samuel yelled, "Look out!" As I turned, a mountain of a wave broke on top of us, and being side on, flipped us straight over. The chill of the water was like an electric shock and instinctively I held my breath whilst being tossed over and over by the wave - like being in a washing machine. I thrashed my arms to try and swim up to the surface, but became disorientated, and couldn't tell if I was going up or down. My heart was beating faster and faster and I felt the blood rushing through my head. My lungs were starting to burn and the urge to try and breathe in was almost unbearable.

A million thoughts a second were flooding through my mind. Was I about to meet my maker? Is this it, was I going to drown in the Atlantic Ocean whilst in a time warp? "Dref, you fish-faced alien jerk, this is all your fault! Where the hell are you when I need you? For god's sake get me out of this hell!"

Momentarily, I surfaced, gasped a breath then the next second…whoosh! I was forced back under again, into the washing machine. Then with a sickening crack, I came to an abrupt halt and surfaced once again, snatching a lungful of air, feeling a surge of relief that at last I'd beached. I tried to sit up and take stock of my surroundings but discovered my leg was stuck fast between two rocks. As each wave washed over me, I could feel the skin being taken off my shin as if by a cheese grater. I pushed, pulled, twisted and turned in desperation and with the help of the slime popping out of the seaweed, eventually managed to struggle free and scrabble further up the rocks away from the waves that were breaking all around me.

I crawled onto a small plateau, looked around me and realised that I hadn't reached the shore at all. I was on an outcrop of rock, not much bigger than my front garden back home, and I was still about half a mile from the original island that we had landed on. I heard a snorting sound and turned around hoping to see Dref again, but instead I was startled to come face to face with an enormous bull seal, and what must have been several other members of his family as surprised to see me as I was them! They quickly turned and slithered silently beneath the waves.

Whilst beginning to shake uncontrollably from the effects of the cold wet clothes that were hanging on me, I tried to gather my thoughts and survey the scene around me, hoping that I could at least find Dref, for without him my prospects were starting to look very grim indeed! From my temporary rock perch, I could now see the full extent of the terrible disaster that we had been unfortunate enough to land in the middle of. The surrounding waters were literally peppered with outcrops of rocks sticking out of the water like stone teeth. In the distance were the wrecks of three maybe four sailing ships, and their contents and remains seemed to be floating on the surface, churning over in the waves almost as far as the eye could see.

Looking towards the nearest inhabited island, I could just make out a lighthouse. However, did they manage to hit the rocks, with a lighthouse so close? I wondered. But more importantly, lurching up on the waves were three longboats with six or eight men in each and a sail at the rear. Without the sails they would have closely resembled the gigs that I had seen racing at Newquay the previous summer. No doubt they were making their way to the wrecks to claim a share of the booty before the excise men laid claim to it. I was just wondering whether or not Sammy Murphy made it to the shore, when out of the corner of my eye I noticed a figure struggling in the water between me and the island. Yes, it was Murphy alright, but he looked almost done in.

I dived back into the icy water, but with the combination of the numbing effect of the cold and the swirling current, progress was extremely slow.

I swam for what seemed like hours, but Murphy appeared to be still afloat, aided by a huge length of planking from one of the wrecks. I was nearing exhaustion and my legs no longer felt like they belonged to me. I was startled by a huge smooth slimy thing rising up from underneath me. It was Dref. I grabbed hold of his dorsal fin, and the next second we were skittering through the water faster than I had ever travelled in a speedboat. I was shouting obscenities at Dref, cursing him for disappearing when I needed him most, and at the same time giving him instructions where to go. Within minutes we reached the shallows of the islands. I half crawled, half walked up the beach, totally exhausted. Dref, meanwhile, formalized back into human form as he left the water and strode up the beach as if he had just stepped out of the shower, totally refreshed! He was starting to annoy me!

“Well, Andy, what are we going to do next? That last idea of yours was not very smart. It’s no good trying to rescue anyone else when we don't even know how we're going to save ourselves. Unless we work as a team we'll never get out of here and it certainly doesn't help when you have evil thoughts about me!"

"What do you mean?" I retorted, with anger and frustration welling up inside me.

"Calling me a fish-faced alien jerk isn't exactly very friendly. We Mondernians communicate mainly by telepathy. We do not have a use for telephones or radios as a means of communication like you Earth people do. That's how I knew what the girls were thinking when we were having our meal at your house."

Suddenly, I felt just like the girls must have done - embarrassed! In addition to that, I felt ashamed and a little inadequate.
"I think we should at least try and get that poor Murphy fellow back on dry land, don't you think so, Dref? Perhaps you could go out and bring him in the same as you did me?"

Dref looked perplexed. "Why should you want to help someone who has tried to overpower you once already? At home, hostile creatures are sent into an ever-widening orbit in a trash capsule!"

I was fast beginning to realise that the natives of Mondern had totally different values to those of us on Earth.
“Here we do things differently, Dref. We are more inclined to forgive and forget. After all, he only acted in the manner he did because he was frightened.”

Looking even more bemused. “Frightened!” Dref exclaimed. “I do not understand this term ‘frightened’ but what I do know is that if I had not come to your aid, you would have er ... past your sell-by date as they say. Then you too would have gone into never ending orbit in the trash capsule!”

“Mmm,” I thought, “burials in space. Now there’s an innovative idea!”

Dref mellowed, and agreed to go and bring Murphy in, but made it quite plain that he didn’t like him and was only doing it because I asked him to. He was bowing to human customs and values, strange though he thought they were!

As he walked back down into the water, he started to formalize back into dolphin mode. Starting with the head, then his shoulders and arms, by the time he was knee deep the transformation was almost complete. As he dived into the waves, his legs and feet became one, to form a tail fin. I didn't think I would ever get used to seeing him transform like that. It was eerie yet fascinating.

Whilst Dref was rescuing Murphy, I decided to walk around to the next cove to see how the other survivor was that we had left on the beach. The cove was strewn with debris from the wrecks. It was hard to take in the enormity of the disaster. There were tons of splintered wood riding in on the waves; as they broke it looked like the sea was throwing back unwanted items, as the wood tumbled over and mixed with clothes, sailcloth, ropes and other personal effects. The gulls circling overhead were spoilt for choice. They chattered away, and every so often swooped down in unison on scraps of food from the doomed ship's stores that were floating in on the flotsam and jetsam.

The wind was still keen but there were a few breaks starting to appear between the clouds. As the sun broke through, I turned the corner into the next cove. The survivor was gone. The tide had gone out, so he couldn't have been dragged back out to sea. He must have gained consciousness and wandered off. I ran through the long grass and up over the sand dunes to a vantage point. From here I could see most of the island, and he was nowhere to be seen. But on the next hillock were the remains of a stone cottage - maybe he was sheltering in there?

Before going to investigate, I thought it was best to go back to the beach and wait for Dref and Murphy. As I climbed the rock that separated the bay from the cove, I could hear the young Irishman shouting at the top of his voice, “Whoa, whoa, yer idjut fish, stop, stop!” There was Murphy holding onto the plank of wood, as if he were in a surfing competition. Dref’s nose was pushed up against the end, and he was propelling it through the water at great speed.

When they were about twenty yards from the beach, Dref’s body lifted out of the water; as he turned, his tail came down on the end of the plank and catapulted poor old Murphy headfirst into the water. Dref swam off towards the cove. Samuel Murphy picked himself up out of the sea, still shouting after the fish that he was fast developing a love hate relationship with. “Thanks for nothin’ yer big slimy idjut, just wait till I get me hands on yer!”

“Don’t be too hard on him, Sam. At least he got you back to the beach, and you couldn’t have done that on your own.”

“Ah reckon I was doing okay,” Murphy replied, trying to salvage his pride. “I was busy paddling away, mindin’ me own business and I would’ve gotten here eventually, when all of a sudden, the idjut fish smacks his nose into the back o’ me board, and the next ting I know, I'm keelhauled! But it never really bothered me, it wasn't the first time I've been adrift on a lump o' wood, and I doubt if it'll be the last!"

I couldn't help smiling at his blustery manner. Here was a chap, same age as me almost but in a different time, who probably faced more life or death situations in a week than I under normal circumstances would face in most of my life. But he was obviously going to take this situation all in his stride. I suggested that we go and look for the other survivor who he may well know, and we set off across the beach, heading firstly towards the remains of the old stone cottage up on the hill.

We had only gone a few hundred yards when Murphy exclaimed, "Is dat who yer mean, him climbing over dat rock der?!"

Momentarily, I thought it was, but when I looked harder, I realised it was Dref. He must have swum around to the cove so that Murphy wouldn't see him formalizing, and then dressed himself in some of the clothes that were being washed up from the wrecks so that he blended in more credibly with the surroundings. I immediately realised that Dref must have read my mind telepathically, because only moments beforehand when I saw Murphy crawling out of the water, I looked at his clothes and thought that if Dref and I could possibly find some clothes floating in the water then it might be an idea to grab them and lay them on the rocks to dry so that we could at least keep warm. Heaven knows how long it was going to take for us to get out of this nightmare.

"No, that's not him, Sam, that's Dref, a friend that came from the island with me."

"How many more of yer are there?" Sam asked, looking threatened once again.

"There's only the two of us and of course the fish," I said reassuringly.

"Der less said about dat idjut der better," scowled Murphy.

Oh my gosh, I thought, if he carries on like that he and Dref will end up having a punch up, especially as Dref appears to be telepathic as well. I'd better give Dref in dolphin-mode a name. The most logical name that sprang to mind was Fred, which was an anagram of Dref.

"It would be sensible if you stopped talking about the fish - who is actually called Fred - in that manner before Dref gets here,

Sam, because he is even more attached to him than me, and Dref is very quick tempered. You don't really want to be crossing him!"

Murphy just grunted to acknowledge what I had said. I think he'd had enough shocks for one day, and so off he went along the beach and up over the hill looking for more seagulls' eggs to make his long-awaited omelette.

CHAPTER 5

After splitting up and searching the island thoroughly, we came to the conclusion that the other survivor had either been picked up by one of the gigs, tried to swim to another island, or maybe even to one of the upturned boats.

Murphy came back up the hill with his hat full of gull eggs. We resigned ourselves to the fact that we were going to be stuck on the island for the night or maybe several nights and we worked out a list of priorities. Firstly, we had to light a fire. No matches of course, so we had to resort to primitive tactics; rubbing two sticks together until they started to smoulder and then blow on the red embers to try and produce a flame and throwing some dry grass on it. First time, no luck. Second time, no luck!! Third time, hey presto it worked!

We soon had a roaring fire going but realised that we would have to let it die down a bit or whatever we tried to cook would just be incinerated! Whilst this was happening, we decided to scour the beach again for any old pots and pans that may have been washed ashore from the wrecks. Dref snuck off to the north beach, I suspect to do a spot of fishing to supplement the gulls' eggs. As Murphy and I rounded the cove we met with the sickening sight of four bloated bodies washed up on the shingle bank. As I turned over the body nearest to me, I cast my eyes upon the most grotesque sight imaginable and promptly threw up. The face was half eaten away by crabs and there were great fat lugworms oozing out of the sand filled eye sockets.

I turned to shout at Murphy and out of the corner of my eye I thought I was seeing things; there he was rifling through the pockets of one of the other corpses. I flung myself across the beach and pulled him off.

"Whoa ya big idjut, what the hell doya tink you're doin?"

"Have some respect for the dead for heaven's sake you pathetic moron," I retorted.

"Respect," Murphy snarled. "Respect, poor old Albert'll ha' no use for this where he's gone, but I certainly have ya gert softee."

With that he flicked open the cutthroat he had just taken off the body and quick as a flash lunged at my face. I instinctively leaned back as the cold steel flashed past my face but nevertheless it still nicked my cheek! He was coming at me again and without thinking about it my foot swung up and caught him straight in the crotch. As he doubled over, I rabbit punched him on the back of the neck, he sprawled across the shingle, I kicked him in the ribs for good measure, grabbed the blade and flung it as far as I could.

He was almost out for the count; I dragged him away from the corpses and sat him up to talk some sense and decency into him as Dref came jumping over the sand dune in human form.
"Hey, you two, stop fooling around and give me a hand with this dinghy I've found over the other side!" Dref exclaimed, "What are these ex-humans doing laying around? If this were on Mondern we would have transported them to the great unknown in a trash capsule by now. What are you going to do, bury them or leave them there to putrefy?"

"Well, funny you should say that Dref. Our friend Murphy here was just robbing the bodies!"

"Dinna be so soft, you big idjut whelp! Where I come from, we live by the rule 'finders' keepers' and it don't matter whether they be dead or alive, so climb off my case softee or I'll skin yer alive at the first opportunity."

I could see we were going to have problems with Murphy; what I was forgetting was that he was from a different time and place than me or Dref, with very different values and priorities, the main one I suppose being survival. Having said that, here I was, also with an alien from another world, who was as different again at the other end of the spectrum! What a weird situation! We had to get back to civilisation wherever that is, or one of us was surely going to perish if we stayed there much longer.

I turned to Murphy, "C'mon get up off your backside, we're going to help Dref with this boat. It might just enable us to get off this island."

"The sooner that the better, then we split. I've had enough of yous ya big sis!" growled Murphy. "And while we're at it, you can call me Mr. Murphy or just plain Sam, but stop calling me plain Murphy, it's disrespectful and moreover reminds me of my skipper keepin' on at me all a time…do this Murphy, do that Murphy. Dus yous get my drift?"

I chose to ignore the remark and looked at Dref who was getting more impatient by the second. "Okay, where is this boat then? We'll have to come back with some planks of wood when we've done the boat thing and bury these poor blighters."

Dref was eager to show us his find and we duly followed him up over the dune and trudged through the marram grass to the other side of the island. When the beach came into view, I couldn't believe my eyes - there tied to a rock was a nine-seater gig in almost perfect condition, complete with oars and rowlocks stowed under the seats.

“Wow, Dref, where did you find this?”

“It was floating about ten ship lengths out; I grabbed the rope that was trailing in the water and swam in with it! Do you think it will be useful?”

“Useful? I should say so, we can row the few miles across to that other island where the lighthouse is!”

“Aye, an’ I can finally be rid o’ yous both,” chimed in Murphy.

“Well so be it, but for now we have to put our differences to one side and literally pull together so as we don’t all end up as stiffs on the beach like those other poor souls!”

But in the back of my mind, I knew deep down that would only be the fate of me and Murphy, as Dref with his ‘special powers’ could carry on swimming around in the sea if necessary. But he still had to make contact with his own people at some stage, although that was the least of our problems right now.

"Talking about stiffs, we had better go back over the other side and try and bury those poor guys before the seagulls start pecking at them. Grab some of those short planks that have been washed up over there we can use them as shovels."

"Don't talk to me about shovel," barked Murphy. "He's the daf' begger that sailed us into the rocks."

That was the first time Murphy had tried to be funny, albeit black humour! We trudged back across to the other side of the island.

Murphy shrieked, "They've gone, they've gone."

I thought he'd finally taken leave of his senses but looking up and down the beach he was right; they were nowhere to be seen, or had we come to the wrong beach?

Dref echoed my thought: "Are you sure this is the right spot, or have you got it wrong?"

"No way," replied Murphy before I could open my mouth. "This is the spot alright. I recognise that pile of kelp there."

I suddenly had visions of zombies marching up the beach towards us. I had the unnerving feeling that we were no longer alone on this island. For a few moments nobody spoke; we were taken aback by the illogical disappearance of four bodies!

“Hey, look there,” exclaimed Murphy. “That there’s a cart track, someun ’as bin here an’ loaded ’em up. C’mon let’s go find ’em.”

We followed the track for about twenty yards or so then lost it once we got into the grass.

Dref said, “There’s no point in just standing here, let’s split up and search the island.”

Murphy and I looked at each other and we were both thinking the same thing: there is safety in numbers, but it made sense to split up and cover the island quicker so that we could find out exactly what we were dealing with. I suggested we let out an owl hoot if we came across anything.

“Okay, there’s no point in going back the way we’ve just come, so I’ll follow the beach around to the other side of the cove. Murphy, you go east over the other side of that hill, and Dref you take the hill to the west, but remember no heroics. If you see anything, lay low and give out the hoot, then wait until we can join you."

Off we went, each of us apprehensive to say the least, although Dref didn't seem particularly phased by any of these strange goings on. I had no sooner rounded the headland of the cove, out of sight of the others, when I heard a very lifelike owl hoot being repeated and getting closer. I looked up and there was in fact an enormous barn owl swooping down and coming straight for me. It came down and landed right next to me. Straightaway it started formalizing; I should have known it was Dref!

"Well, what have you found then?"

"I was going to practice an owl hoot; it must have been good because I formalized into one! But that made it much easier to scan the island and I discovered an old stone building right over the other side at the furthest point tucked in behind some big bushes in a small hollow and there is a very ancient female humanoid dancing around the four ex humanoids in a very strange fashion."

In one sense I could not believe what Dref was telling me, but on the other hand I did remember learning in history about witches being banished to uninhabited islands or in some cases even being burnt at the stake. So, it was feasible that what Dref was telling me was right. Wary though I was of possibly being turned into a frog if we approached the old woman, I was taking comfort from the fact that Dref's extraordinary powers were probably superior to that of hers! We were about to find out.

"C'mon then, Dref. Let's go find Murphy and the three of us will go and see what this is all about."

Dref looked apprehensive. "Do you think that's wise? Murphy is from these times and is both suspicious and superstitious. Seeing that situation may just push him over the top and he'll totally lose it. Perhaps we should go and check it out first, don't you think?"

"Putting it like that I've got to agree with you. Come on then, let's do it."

As we were walking over the hill towards what Dref had identified, there seemed to be an awkward silence between us. "Are you feeling nervous?" I asked.

"No," replied Dref. "But as we are getting closer to the old woman's place, I have some strange signals coming into my head, and they are not all good ones either!"

Sure enough, as we approached the tumbledown cottage, we could hear the monotonous chanting and a pungent smell filled the air, seemingly coming from an old cauldron that was hanging from a tripod above a roaring fire. She was chanting as she was stirring whatever was cooking and every now and then she flicked some of the gruel off the spoon across the bodies lined up on the grass beside her. Suddenly, but slowly, the bodies started to stand and take on zombie-like features. The eye sockets were empty, and the skin was hanging off in shreds. The old woman was obviously a witch and that probably was the reason she was banished to an off-island. She seemed to have control over the bodies, her head was bowed, and she was chanting some indecipherable cantor. As she lifted her head her eyes settled directly on us, and she instantly shrieked a blood curling obscenity whilst directing the zombies towards us.

If that wasn't bad enough, at the same time, Murphy came charging over the hill, ran straight past and launched himself at the old woman in the style of a rugby tackle. She stepped deftly to one side, pointed her bony finger at him and spat out what sounded like a curse and instantaneously poor old Murphy became a writhing snake that she snatched up from the ground and threw into the pot. Dref and I looked at each other and realised the grotesque zombies were almost upon us. We took to our heels and charged back up the hill; she was still screaming after us, obviously determined to stop us, and around our feet the ivy trailing across the ground started moving and lifting off the ground trying to wrap around our ankles.

As the north beach came into view, there appeared to be another gig pulled up on the beach next to ours and there were six soldiers in scarlet jackets with muskets at the ready running towards us. Speechless, we pointed back to where we had just come from. They took the hint and charged off down towards the old hag and the zombies and whatever was left of Murphy. They asked no questions, they just opened fire. The old woman's head exploded like a ripe melon, and the zombies shredded and collapsed to the ground as their guiding power was extinguished. The lead soldier hooked his boot under the old woman and turned her over as if to make sure she was no longer a threat, whilst another tipped the pot over off the tripod. The contents spilled on the ground, together with the snake. I expected to see Murphy come back to life as a human, but it was not to be, he was well and truly cooked!

Whilst the soldiers were busy with the old hag and the remains of Murphy, we thought that it was a good time to scarper. We made it over the top of the hill and as we were running down towards the beach, we heard shouting from the militia; they had obviously noticed that we were gone.

“C’mon, Dref, faster or they will fill us with lead once they get over the top of that hill!”

Just then, the most enormous albatross flew overhead. That must have given Dref an idea, and within seconds he had transformed into the very same bird and was running alongside beckoning me to climb on his back. By now the militia had come over the hill and had started firing at us. Luckily, we were out of range, but not for long. I leapt on Dref’s back and with another ten paces he was flapping his wings and we were airborne! I looked back at the militia, and they had stopped dead in their tracks and naturally couldn’t believe their eyes.

Wow! This is fantastic, I thought. Within seconds we were several hundred feet above the waves. I could see for miles, and it looked like there were dozens of small islands, but nearest to us was a larger one that looked inhabited, or at least it had what looked like a lighthouse a short way back from the shoreline, and I guessed that was where Dref was taking us. With the wind blowing through my hair, it felt like I was on the most fantastic roller coaster ever. A few gulls and guillemots tried to keep up with us, but they had no chance; we must have doing over fifty miles an hour.

Suddenly, disaster struck! Dref's head started to transform back into human and, oh my, he was beginning to look half human, half bird, and we were losing height rapidly.

I shouted in panic. "Dref, what's happening?"

"I don't know! My formalization seems to be wearing off. I can't keep us up much longer. I'll try and get us as close to land as I can, without diving into the rocks!"

Then that was it, his wings became arms, his tail feathers became legs again and we were both diving headfirst towards the rocks.

I managed to twist my body enough to alter the angle of descent and seconds later we both hit the water which luckily was quite deep, even though when we surfaced, we were only about one hundred yards from the beach. We struck out for the shore and wow, Dref could swim like a fish even though he was still in human form. As we neared the shoreline, we were swept up on the giant rollers that were coming in, and in seconds we were dumped on the white sand, and we scrabbled furiously to get far enough up the beach so as not to get dragged back in.

CHAPTER 6

We were both laying on the rocks further up the beach, trying to catch our breath as we heard footsteps crunching across the shingle. I looked up and nudged Dref, thinking maybe it was militia men again like we encountered on the other island.

To our surprise it turned out to be a couple of fair-haired girls, one about the same age as us and the other, possibly her sister judging by the looks, about two years younger.

"Well, well, look what we've found!" exclaimed the older one. "A couple of half dead water rats been washed up, from the wrecks I suppose. What do you think, Maisy, shall we beat 'em over the head and put 'em out of their misery or go and get Dad to bring the cart down and load 'em up, he may be able to find a use for 'em?"

"No need to get a cart," I said. "We can walk."

I started to stand up, whilst at the same time trying to give Dref a hand up; he seemed totally wiped out.

"No, stay right where you are," screamed the elder girl. "We have strict orders not to let any of you scabby disease-ridden sailors off the beach until you been examined. We don't want you infecting us all here. Maisy, you stay here. If they move, start screaming and lob these small rocks at them. I'll go get our Dad now; he's only lifting spuds in over there in Jim's field."

"What do you think, Dref, shall we wait for their old man or make a run for it?"

"Andy, get real, we have just landed on another island. Where are we going to run to, back into the sea?"

Before I could answer, the girl reappeared dragging behind her a man mountain, who I assumed was her father.

"Well you lads, my name is John Pender," he boomed. "If you give me any trouble, I'll tie you up in the barn and you can stay there until the boat comes to get you both and take you back to St.Mary's. But if you behave yourselves, I could do with a couple of extra pairs of hands until they fetch you. So, it's all up to you two. What's it going to be then?"

Dref spoke first to my surprise in a broad west country accent!

“Well, sir, that’s very kind of you, we will do whatever you require. What’s our first task?”

“There are still a few bodies of your shipmates washed up around the corner in the cove; they need loading on the trailer and taking down to the church. We’re having to use it as a mortuary at the moment. Never seen so many corpses in all me life, hardly any survivors, don’t know how you lads managed it, just lucky I suppose!”

I was right on the verge of puking up thinking about loading up corpses, when a great rock landed on the back of my head.

“Maisy,” bellowed the old man. “Leave ’em be, no point in damaging ’em, they won’t be worth as much!”

Before I could gather my thoughts, which were a bit muddled anyway from the bang on the head, and the thought of ‘not worth as much’…what was he planning on doing, selling us? The old man started bellowing, “C’mon then, let’s be having you, we’ve got bodies to move.”

Yuk yuk yuk!

We followed the father and two giggling daughters up the long and winding stony track from the beach. We climbed up and over a small hillock and followed the old man into a small cart shed.

"There you go, hitch up that there cart one on each side and follow me down to Shell Bay. That's where most of the bodies are washed up, and we need to move 'em before the rats get at 'em!"

"You girls scoot off home and help your Ma get the dinner. Tell her there'll be two more mouths to feed."

Dragging the cart empty was bad enough, what's it going to be like with a load of bodies on it? As we approached the beach, even from a hundred yards away we could smell the death. Dref was looking none too happy and hadn't said a word since we left the beach on the other side of the island. I just hope he was busy figuring out how we were going to get back to our own time and place. We started loading the corpses - Mr. Pender lifted them up under the arms and Dref and I took a leg each. They were all in a bad way, bloated with the seawater and beaten about from being washed on to the rocks. This was not a pleasant task! Dref and I were both retching as we heaved the slippery corpses up onto the trailer. Having loaded up six, which was all the trailer could take, I said to Dref, "We're never going to pull that!"

Mr. Pender must have overheard me, and to our relief he said, "You lads wait here while I go and fetch Bess and harness her up. Make sure nobody runs off!" And he went off up the track chuckling to himself at his own black humour!

Suddenly, the trailer started rocking and shaking and there were deathly groaning sounds coming from the middle of it. Dref and I looked at each other, thoroughly petrified. Then without any further warning, what looked like a giant groaning zombie started to emerge from under the heap of bodies. Just then, Mr. Pender came back over the headland with Bess.

"Whoa, what's'a goin' on 'ere then? Ha ha, we got ourselves a live one I see!"

Wow, that was a relief at least to know it wasn't a real live zombie!

"Well, give the poor begger a hand down you lads, don't just stand there gawking at him." The old black-bearded sailor didn't need much help in getting off the cart, he swayed and he roared.

“I am bosun Baines of the good ship Charlotte. Get me down from here, these corpses stink!” And with that he slipped on the slime and fell headfirst off the cart flat onto his face!
He looked like he was dead, he never moved a muscle, but old man Pender ran over, unhooked a bucket off the front of the cart, scooped some water up from the sea and threw it over the head of bosun Baines. With that he shook and coughed and spluttered, then tried to get up but promptly fell straight back down again! Dref and I couldn’t stop laughing despite the horror of the situation, much to the dismay of Mr. Pender.

“I told you two to help him,” he bellowed. “Get over there and give him a lift up.”

With that, a size ten boot caught us both up our backsides and propelled us at speed towards Baines. We did manage to stand him up this time, and as wobbly as he was, he managed to stay up. Pender came over and hooked his arm under him and started off up the track. He looked back over his shoulder. “You two good for nothing squirts, lead Bess up the track behind me. When we get to the cottage, you carry on round to the churchyard and wait there for me while I sort this ’un out.”

Bess was a cantankerous old nag and she didn’t see why she should move for us; we pulled her, pushed her, shouted at her, spoke nicely to her, but she wasn't going to move. Out of the corner of my eye I thought I saw the head of another horse, but no, it was Dref formalizing into a beautiful stallion and he started frolicking and cantering up and down the track ahead of us!

Sure enough Bess started to move and slowly the cart started rolling along behind her. Dref, being forever the clown, continued the act all the way down to the churchyard, then became himself once again. Bess just looked at him and cocked her head looking as confused as an animal could possibly look!

There were several other carts drawn up next to the churchyard with corpses dangling off the sides. The vicar was shuffling around mumbling and genuflecting. It was a bizarre and sorrowful sight - all these poor dead sailors, many of them not much more than boys of my own age and no one here to mourn them. Dref was looking very thoughtful. I looked at him enquiringly.

"I can fix this!" he exclaimed.

"What do you mean? Fix what?" I asked.

"These guys are not dead, they're just waterlogged!"

“Ha ha,” I laughed out loud. Much to the dismay of the vicar and other folks who had started to arrive, I pretended I was crying at the dreadful scene, but I don’t think I was very convincing! I could see from the look on Dref’s face that he wasn’t about to tell me something funny.

“I’m being serious,” he said. “Back at home on Mondern when this happens to people, we can ask the son of Sun God to send a concentrated beam of heat directly onto the victims and in seconds the water is drawn out of them, and they are like brand new again.”

“Is that so?” I said cynically. “Well, for one thing we are not on planet Mondern and for another thing, I bet it didn’t work all the time, did it?”

“Well, maybe we did get it wrong every now and then and end up frying a few, but most of them were ok! If I could get somewhere quiet for a few minutes and use all my telepathic power, I might just be able to do something!”

I really didn’t know what to think or say. Part of me was thinking if there’s a chance it could work let’s go for it. And the other part of me was thinking that if it was to go wrong, we would probably get burnt at the stake for practising witchcraft. I'd read somewhere that they still did that in the early 18th century! But the reckless part of me won.

"C'mon then, quick let's get around the back of the church before old Pender turns up."

Around the back in the churchyard several graves had already been dug ready to receive the bodies. As we passed the one nearest to us, we noticed that there was already a body in the bottom wrapped in a shroud, waiting to be covered over. Dref sat down leaning against an extra-large headstone and went into a ghostly like trance, his eyes rolled into the top of his head, and he started to convulse. I did not like this one little bit. Then suddenly, the sun appeared to get extremely bright for a few seconds and its rays seemed to be concentrated straight into the bottom of the hole where the body was laying. For a few seconds, it started hissing and popping and steam started to rise up and the shroud was turning brown, and then, oh my god, it started writhing and turning and rising up. Dref snapped out of his trance, we both looked at each other and ran!

We opened a door at the side of the church which led us into the vestry where the vicar kept his gowns.

“It worked, it worked!” Dref blurted out excitedly.

“Yes, but what sort of a state is he going to be in?”
“How would I know?” replied Dref. “But it least it worked. Let’s see if we can do the others!”

Wow, I thought, this really is one crazy alien! Just then we heard the door open at the other end of the church. “What are we going to do now? We can’t get caught in here.”

There was another door in the corner of the vestry, I ran over and opened it, and found there was a staircase which presumably led up to the bell tower. I beckoned to Dref to follow in behind me. There was a bolt on the inside which I slid across, just in case anyone heard us and was about to follow. We ran up the stairs three at a time, which was difficult as they were spiral. At the top it opened out into a small room with the rope bells hanging down in the middle. There was a small gap in the tower where a window should have been. I looked through it and had a fantastic view of not only down below but all the surrounding area.

“Hey Dref, come and have a look at this.”

We could see the three carts with the bodies loaded on directly below us and there walking down the track, a few hundred yards away, was old Pender. I looked again at Dref.

“I’ve got to do this now,” he declared, and before I could say anything, he slid down against the wall and went back into his trance. Within seconds as the cloud was clearing, a wide beam of hot bright sunlight, even though it was October, shone down and spread across the three carts with the bodies on. About a minute passed and the carts started shaking and the bodies started to steam and fidget. The villagers backed away and cowered behind the churchyard wall and the headstones. Then one by one the corpses were untangling themselves and trying to stand. The sun was still beating down, and they were frying, their skin was hanging off them and their ragged clothes were smouldering. Dref was still in a trance, he had to stop. “Dref, stop now!” He took no notice, he was convulsing and foaming at the mouth.

I dived over and shook him and whacked him on the arm. He snapped out of it and looked at me as if I were crazy! By now I could hear terrified screams and shouts coming from down below. We looked out of the gap in the wall and the scene we saw can only be described as pure chaos!

Instead of corpses, we now had zombies half climbing, half falling off the carts, then wandering around clearly not knowing who they were what they were or where they were!

People were running in all directions, panic stricken. The vicar was on his knees looking up to heaven and obviously praying for forgiveness. Maybe he was blaming himself thinking that he had said the wrong prayer in the first place!

We looked out of the gap the other side and we could see that the first one Dref had experimented on had managed to climb out of the grave and was staggering off towards the beach. He really did look drunk. Dref suddenly started laughing.

"I think I did quite well really!" Dref exclaimed. "They won't have to dig all those holes now to bury them. I think that's a daft idea anyway, most unhygienic. We would put them in trash capsules and blast them off to infinity. Don't you remember I told you that before? Anyway, the good news is now that I've made contact telepathically, we may actually be able to get ourselves out of here!"

CHAPTER 7

After Dref had worked his magic on the remaining corpses, we thought we had better make ourselves scarce as we had just unleashed the ghastly zombie sailors on the unsuspecting island community. We ran off towards the beach and gradually the screams and shouts from the locals faded into the distance.

We walked on around the coastline looking for somewhere decent to hide out while we planned our next move. Dref seemed to have a new spring in his step since his success with the zombies and I was starting to wonder what he was going to come up with next.

The beach was starting to get very rocky and suddenly we came across a family of seals basking in the sun. Momentarily they were startled; the adult ones turned and were about to slither back into the sea but suddenly stopped and turned. I glanced at Dref and sure enough he was formalizing into a seal and within seconds was flapping across the rocks to join his new friends. They didn't look too chuffed about him to start with and were starting to get quite aggressive, but they soon calmed down and even appeared to be welcoming their new friend.

Suddenly, they all turned and disappeared into the water like a team of synchronised swimmers, and I was left standing on the rock all alone, once again wondering what was going to happen next. For the next hour or so Dref was performing the most amazing aquatic tricks with his new friends - showing off, most people would call it. One minute they were there, the next minute they were all gone. Probably they spotted a shoal of fish and decided it was feeding time. Dref was left sitting alone on the rock and after a few minutes slithered back into the water and back over to me. As soon as he was out of the water, he began to change back into human form again.

“Those creatures are pretty dumb!” he exclaimed.

“Why’s that?” I asked.

“Well, I was trying to teach them some tricks, but they didn’t want to join in, and they couldn’t communicate either!”

“I reckon they thought you were an imposter and they just let you entertain them until they got bored. Anyway, getting back to more serious stuff, you said you had contacted your people. What happens next?”

“If we can get a really fierce fire going somewhere, they may be able to pick us out with their heat seeker and beam us up.”

“The lighthouse just across the bay!”

“What about it?” asked Dref.

“The lighthouse has a fire basket which is lit at night, that’s what warns the ships out at sea,” I explained. “If we were to volunteer to stoke it one night, then that might produce enough energy for your mothership to pick up on if you think it’s in the area, and the keepers are always looking for volunteers to cart the wood and coal up the to the top. I read about that in history at school. Come on, let’s swim over to it.”

CHAPTER 8

Dref made it to the beach a few minutes before me and was already up looking over the grassy sand dunes by the time I made landfall. I scrambled up the sand and joined Dref who was smiling to himself.

"What are looking so smug about? You almost crashed us into the rocks back there. That would have made a right old mess of us!" I said.

"So what, we didn't did we?" Dref replied looking at the old lighthouse out on the peninsula. "What you see there is what is going to get us out of here!"

"How's that then? If the keeper is there, he'll run us off the island."

"No chance of that," Dref declared. "It looks deserted to me. Come on, let's go and have a look!"

We made our way up the small hillock towards the lighthouse. Sure enough, when we got there it did look deserted; the big oak door at the bottom was swinging freely, so we pushed it open and started to climb the spiral stone staircase. I decided to count the steps. We got to one hundred and two and that was it, we couldn't go any further, and there was an old iron trap door above us. I turned to Dref, "Hey, give me a hand, see if we can shove this up!"

No sooner had we started pushing, then it was ripped out of our hands and standing there was a wrinkled and whiskery old lighthouse keeper. "What the devil are you doing here?" he bellowed. I fell back onto Dref and we both nearly went tumbling back down the spiral staircase, but Dref managed to grab the rail and somehow managed to support the both of us. My brain went into overdrive, and I didn't want to get on the wrong side of the keeper.

"Good afternoon, sir. We've been sent over to help you stock the brazier for the night." I quickly stuttered. I had remembered from my history lessons at school that before electric lights were used the lighthouses were lit by coal contained in an iron holder known as a brazier.

"Well, you're a bit late. They said they were sending a couple of lads up three days ago. I've been struggling real bad with me back and all, but seeing as you're here now you'd just as well get started, follow me up and get the baskets."

Dref and I looked at each other and without saying a word looked back at the keeper and nodded as he turned to make his way back up the spiral staircase.

"Well, I'll be darned!" exclaimed the old keeper. "I've been asking for a lad to help for weeks since I done my back in, now two of you have turn up, how about that!"

I nearly said, "Just like the buses," but I checked myself at the last second when I remembered that the internal combustion engine hadn't been invented yet, let alone buses!

"You'd better come on up then the pair of you."

So far so good, I thought! Dref meanwhile hadn't said a word, but all that was about to change!

"I'm Dref and this is my friend, Andy. May I ask your name, sir?"

"Of course, son. Bill's my name, Bill Foulkes. I been manning this tower since I was your age. That's fifty years near on now. There you are, there's the baskets over in the corner there, grab one each and get started. It'll probably take you both all day and half the night as you've got nearly two tonnes to haul up to keep the light going for the next couple of days and nights as there's a bank of fog about to roll in later in the day."

We each grabbed a basket, and boy they were heavy without any coal in; they were made of cast iron! Dref seemed to pick his up as if it were made of paper, so I took a deep breath and followed him back down the stairs. I was worried that with the weight of the basket and the steepness of the stairs that I was going to topple over right on top of Dref! The coalhouse wasn't hard to find, it was just across the courtyard, and the coal was spilling out into the yard.

"I suppose we had better fill these two tonnes up and take them back up to the light." said Dref.

Then I realised, of course, that Dref would have no idea what a tonne was, and he must have thought that was what the baskets were!

"You must be joking; it will take about fifty baskets full for a tonne!"

Dref's face dropped! "Are you kidding me, Andy?"

"No, Dref, I'm not, so we had better get started. Here, grab this shovel, I'll race you!"

That was a pretty daft thing to say really as Dref's work rate was twice that of mine, and that just reminded me that he really is superhuman!

Bill the keeper went off for his lunch and left us to haul the coal. Back and forth we went up and down the spiral staircase hauling our heavy baskets. Before long we were almost unrecognisable; each time we either loaded or emptied the baskets, a great cloud of black dust erupted around us. "I thought you were going to race me?" exclaimed Dref.

"I can shift more than you without even trying!" I boasted, while secretly hoping that Dref would start going twice as fast, which would mean I would only have to shift half as much! Within minutes my plan appeared to be working. Dref had definitely increased his pace and in fact was getting faster and faster and was soon doing three or four trips to my one! I couldn't believe it. By mid-afternoon as Bill the keeper reappeared after his lunch, we were just taking the last two baskets up to the light together. Dref was so black and covered in coal dust that he was unrecognisable, and I guess I probably was as well, although Dref had shifted many times more than I had.

“I told you I would beat you,” Dref declared triumphantly. “In fact, I could probably beat you at everything!”

“Ok, you probably could, but don’t get too cocky about it,” I replied. “Maybe if I came to Mondern I could do a few things better than you!”

“Huh, very funny, but that’s not going to happen, is it?” grunted Dref sarcastically. I felt a bit bad after he said that, as I remembered that Planet Mondern had been all but destroyed duc to contamination by its inhabitants. That’s how Dref came to Earth in the first place, as his family were travelling the solar system looking for an alternative planet to migrate to. It seemed like I had known Dref forever, but in reality, it had only been a few days since the mishap with the battery charger in my Dad’s shed, that had resulted in us waking up way back in time more than two centuries ago amongst a group of islands in the Atlantic Ocean! Which reminded me, that’s why we were here to try and execute our cunning plan to create enough heat and energy from the coal fire to attract attention from Dref’s mother ship, but without burning the lighthouse down!

CHAPTER 9

"How are we going to be able to get the fire hot enough with the keeper there?" That was the question that was going over and over in my mind! However, I need not have worried, as Bill the keeper was very much worse for wear from booze! He had obviously had a liquid lunch at the local tavern and was finding it very difficult to either stand up without wobbling or walk in a straight line!

By the time we got back down to ground level, the keeper had just managed to stagger to the foot of the stairs.

"Hey lads, have you finished that small job that I gave you to do before I left?" With that he threw his head back into a fit of boozy laughter!

"Yes, sir, we've just finished."

"Impossible! The last lads took two days to do that, but it'll be a good job if ya has done it as the fog is coming in and we need to get that brazier lit and hot!"

That was music to our ears!

“Well go and have a look for yourself then,” I said confidently.

“Aye, I will at that. Give ush a hand on these here stairs,” he said slurring his words.

He was taking two steps forward and three steps backwards, so Dref and I took an arm each and helped him up the first few stairs. It all went well until we got to the first bend. Clearly, we were not all three of us going to fit side by side holding him up. We decided to both get behind him and shove. But his weight was too much and that combined with his unsteadiness was a disaster about to happen.

“Where is you lads gone? Hold me, hold me, I’m a gonna fall damn you!”

With that, he let out a tremendous roar like a lion, toppled backwards right over the top of both Dref and I, flattening us in the process, and plunged headlong backwards to the bottom of the staircase and landed in a crumpled, silent heap at the bottom.

“Is he expired?” enquired Dref, almost casually.

I knelt down and felt his pulse. Yes, his heart was still beating and yes, he was still breathing! “No Dref, he’s not expired, just knocked unconscious; he must have taken a bang to the head as he crashed to the bottom. So, we don't need to put him in a trash canister and blast him off into space like your people do! Give me a hand to drag him over and prop him up against that wall. We'll leave him to sleep it off while we go up top and get that fire going!"

I felt a bit sorry for the old keeper, but I doubt it was the first time that he'd had a mishap through drink, and it probably wouldn't be the last! We made our way back up the spiral stairs and once we were at the top, we started to load the brazier with wood and leaves ready to start a small fire before we loaded it with coal. That presented us with our next problem: we had no matches!

"Okay, Dref, how are we going to light this fire then?"

"Andy, you're the native of this world, why are you asking me? But come to think of it, the man Bill had a small fire in front of his mouth, so he must have something here to get that going!"

I wondered for a moment what the heck he was talking about, then I remembered seeing the old keeper puffing away on a clay pipe when he first opened the hatch door to us.

"Hey, Dref, that's good thinking, maybe you are a genius after all!! He must have some matches somewhere; I think in this day and time they called them 'lucifers'. Look around for a box with that written on it. Oh... sorry I forgot, you can't read Earth style lingo, can you?"

I took it from Dref's black look silent response that the answer was no, but he would soon fathom it out! We looked around the office room as it was below the brazier platform but found nothing except for a load of charts and scribbled pieces of paper. Then I remembered that there must be sleeping quarters. There surely must be something in there for lighting his pipe and the brazier. We went down to the next landing and pushed open the big solid oak door. It was very sparse with an iron bedframe and straw mattress with a few blankets chucked on it against one wall, a smelly old cork mat on the floor and an upturned orange box with a cloth on it. Sure enough, sat on the top was old Bill's pipe and baccy with a box of lucifers next to them.

"Hey, Dref, this is what we want. Quick, let's get back upstairs and get that fire roaring like a volcano before the old keeper wakes up from that bang on the head!"

We ran back up the last two flights of steps to the coal brazier, which was a mistake because we should have gone back down to the bottom to pick up some leaves and kindling wood to start a small fire before we started piling the coal on.

“Dref, we’ve got to go back down to the bottom to get some stuff to start the fire off. Quick, follow me!”

“Andy, do you really know what you’re doing? My powerpack is really low now after running up and down with all that black stuff. If I don’t re-energise soon, you’re going to have to put me in the trash capsule.”

“C’mon, Dref, one more trip. I’m sure you can make it, then we can start the fire and put a load of that black stuff on as you call it and I’m sure then that you’ll have a fantastic energy source.”

So, there it was, we found a spare basket in the coal house and had no problem finding enough dead leaves and twigs to fill it up. We crept past old Bill for fear of waking him up, although there wasn’t much chance of that by the look of him; he was still out for the count and snoring loudly.

Dref was really struggling on the last few dozen steps, and I ran on ahead, left the basket at the top and went back to help him up the last few steps and onto the platform. I sat him down on the side as he was really wilting now. I tipped all the dry stuff into the bottom of the brazier and placed a few large lumps of coal on top. I pulled the box of lucifers out of my pocket and took one strike. I teased the flame under the twigs and leaves, and whoosh, it suddenly all ignited and hey presto we were in business. Slowly, as the coals started to catch and glow, I gently started to pile on some more coal and within minutes we had a reasonable fire going. That encouraged Dref to stand up and he came and stood next to me. As the heat began to build up and radiate against his body, he started to return to his normal self.

"Hey, Andy, I guess you've done this before, you've saved me from the trash capsule."

CHAPTER 10

Within minutes, the fire inside the brazier was starting to glow red, and we could now start to really pile on the coal. Dref was starting to toast and had to take a few steps back. It amazed me that something as basic as a good old coal fire could rejuvenate an alien!

"Well done, Andy, if we carry on at this rate then very soon the energy given off from this little lot should start to encourage some inquisitive looks from my people out there! Come on, I'll help you, I'm ok again now. Let's really pile it up; it's our best chance of them picking up a signal!"

We took turns in piling on the coal and within ten minutes it was starting to roar like a blast furnace and was getting hotter and hotter. It's a good job that there was no roof on top like the newer lighthouses or it would certainly have burnt a hole right through the top. I was starting to worry now that the intensity of the heat was actually going to melt the bottom of the brazier basket. But my worries were cut short when I started to feel a vibration and a humming similar to what I had heard the previous week when I fell off my bike in the field. Dref felt it at the same time.

“We’ve done it, we’ve done it!”

Dref was infused with new energy, then suddenly he went into a trance-like state looking up towards the sky and holding his arms up high. In the faint distance as dusk was falling, I could see lights starting to appear in the sky. There was no sound except for the roar of the fire and the gentle humming which was getting louder as the lights were becoming brighter, then the peace was shattered by a thunderous roar.

“What the hell is going on up there? I didn’t tell you to light the damn fire, it’s too early. You were only supposed to take the coal up!”

Bill the keeper had obviously awoken from his booze induced mishap and was already on his way up the spiral staircase, intent on teaching us a lesson. I gave Dref a shove to try and snap him out of his trance.

“Dref, speak to me, the old man’s awake and on his way up the stairs!”

But it was no use, Dref was fixated on the massive object in the sky that was now almost directly above us hovering at about a thousand metres and now it was shining brightly from the rays of the setting sun that were being deflected off the side of it directly down onto Dref who was stood beside me still with his arms outstretched and in a trance. My ears were now starting to ring as the humming changed to a much higher pitch. I could hear Bill still roaring away in spite of the ringing in my ears and he was now only a few steps below us.

With an almighty crash the door flung open, and the lighthouse keeper stood there with his face bright red, in fact, incandescent with rage. He was about to take a swipe at me as I was closest. But at the same time Dref started to levitate, slowly at first, he lifted off the ground with his arms outstretched and then accelerated straight up through the beam into the spacecraft which had an open hatch on the underside. My mind was now racing, I turned to look at Bill who was looking skywards and his face had now turned a deathly white and I thought he was either going to faint or have a heart attack. I was about to say something to him when I was immersed in the same light that covered Dref and I was now filled with a very warm sensation, in fact I thought I was about to pee myself when I too started to lift off the floor, but the next thing I knew I crashed onto a metal floor and I looked up to see Dref and two Dref clones grinning at me!

They both looked like Dref but clearly they were older, and one was male and the other female. I guessed they were his parents, but all three of them including Dref were dressed in the same shiny suits I first saw Dref wearing and who in fact was holding what looked like another suit under his arm.

"Quick, Andy, put this on. We have to get out of here fast, these are my parents by the way."

With that, they both nodded at me and smiled, then disappeared through a sliding door. Dref helped me up and touched a panel on the wall which seemed to activate the closing mechanism for the hatch in the floor. As it closed, I just caught a glimpse of the fire in the brazier burning ferociously and Bill the lighthouse keeper stood beside it with his cap in one hand and scratching his head with the other. He must have been thinking he was either having a terrible dream, or maybe had drunk far too much at lunchtime and was hallucinating!

I turned back to Dref who was looking rather smug.

"Well, what do you think of that, Andy? I said I could get us out of there with a good energy source, didn't I?"

A red light started flashing and at the same time an alarm sounded.

"Quickly now, follow me please," said Dref in a rather formal manner from what I'd been used to from him.

"Why, what's going on?" I asked, panicking a bit in case there was something wrong and we would end up having a lot of explaining to do to old Bill the keeper and many others besides.

"We are just about to power up to light speed. Come through here, take a seat and buckle up the harness. Once we're cruising you can get out and I'll show you around the ship," said Dref in a very matter of fact way!

Once again, I had to pinch myself to make sure that this was really happening, and I wasn't dreaming. Mind you, after all the events of the last week, anything was possible! But this was real alright. It now felt like there was a big hand pushing me back in my seat and the sensation was like being on one of those crazy theme park rides that defies gravity! After a few minutes we levelled off and everything seemed a bit more sedate.

"Okay, you can get out of the harness now," said Dref. "Come on I'll give you a guided tour."

First thing I noticed on my left were two more Dref lookalikes sat at a massive control unit with big television screens in front of them. Directly in front of us were sat the parents in front of what can only be described as a window on the world. We must already have been in the Earth's stratosphere as I could clearly see the curvature of the Earth's surface. But most amazing of all was that there was no sound, no noise whatsoever. In fact, it made me think of a hospital or doctors' waiting room, where everyone speaks or whispers in hushed tones. The other thing was that everything was clinically clean like you would expect in a hospital.

"How come there is no engine noise?" I asked.

"That is because we are solar powered from the star that I believe you call Sun. There are similar sun planets in every galaxy that we pass through and with the panels on the outside of our craft they attract and store the energy. They are ultra-sensitive, and they contain processors that can identify and evaluate any unusual energy source. That's how the mothership was able to track me through the transponder on my belt as I was stood next to the fire that we built up which was a tremendous source of unharnessed energy!"

In the short time that I had known Dref he had always exuded confidence, probably down to the fact that most of the time he was able to revert to his 'special powers' when necessary, which had got us out of quite a few scrapes. But now that he was on his own territory as it were, he was even more confident, with a bit of added maturity. He set about showing me around the craft and introducing me to the other two Dref lookalikes, who turned out to be his brothers and that was the sum total of the occupants, his Mum and Dad and two brothers. There was nothing that Dref wasn't able or prepared to explain to me. It was all so fantastic and futuristic; I was mesmerised by it all.

Dref was in his element, and now in full swing! "This is the accommodation, Andy. You can have this pod next to mine, but it shouldn't be for very long as we are planning on getting you back to your correct time zone, which is a bit complicated because it's not something that we normally do, but we'll do our best; my father is the expert. Which reminds me, I think they both want to have a chat with you about certain things."

That made me a bit apprehensive on several fronts. Firstly, the fact that they didn't usually do the time travel thing. Secondly, what 'things' did they want to talk to me about?

"Dref, we need to talk! Now that we have finally managed to meet up with your mothership I need to know where we go from here, what's going to happen? And you need to tell me more about your world before I speak to your Mum and Dad so as they don't think I'm a total dimwit!"

"Well, as I said to you earlier, Andy, the plan is to get you back to your time and place, but we have a few difficult manoeuvres to carry out first."

"Yes, I understand all that, but what if we overshoot, for example, and end up in the wrong time zone again?"

"Then we deal with it," replied Dref. "What else was it you wanted to know?"

"What really happened before you left Mondern, why can't you ever go back?"

"Like I said to you before, our planet was very similar to your planet Earth, but we were probably several hundred years ahead of yours in technological advancement, which was a good thing in some ways up to a point but then it turned into a bad thing. The reason being that so much attention was being paid to the advancement of space travel and communications with other planets that we started to neglect our own beautiful planet and paying attention to the most basic things like, for example, what we did with our waste products. You remember me saying that when people expired, we would put them in a waste capsule and fire them off into space? Well, that came about because there was no space left to bury them on Mondern which is what happened for hundreds of years, and similarly all our general waste of all descriptions used to get buried in capsules on the planet, but eventually the capsules would deteriorate and burst open, and all the nasty stuff would leak out into the ground and everything around it would become contaminated. Lots of people started dying from mystery illnesses. By lots, I mean thousands, many thousands."

Dref was starting to sound more and more miserable as he was telling his story and I was beginning to feel quite sorry for him. "So why, with all the flash technology could a solution not be found? Why did you have to leave Mondern?"

"Eventually, everything became polluted with toxins that one way or another had got into the food stream either by way of land or water pollution and very few people had resistance to diseases anymore because everything that they ate or drank made them ill, so people started to emigrate to other planets, or at least try and find other planets suitable."

"So, what do you live on whilst you're travelling?" I asked.

"Luckily, some families including ours, of course, managed to stockpile food and liquids over a few years before it all became contaminated. To keep it fresh we super freeze it and then dry it so that when packaged it takes up hardly any space on the craft, but we are starting to run a bit low now! But the problem is, there are a lot of other family craft out there looking for a new home planet, and sometimes they get aggressive and like, we get fired on. In your world I think you would call it 'civil war', but we can handle it, all we have to do is get you back to your time and place and you can then do all the introductions and as you say, 'hey presto' we have a new home planet!"

Dref was starting to worry me now. |It seems like he had it all planned out, but what if his aggressive neighbours decided to follow them to Earth? We could end up with an inter galactic battle right on our doorstep! On top of that I didn't have a great deal of faith in them getting me back to 1965 in one piece. "So, Dref, when are we making the journey back to my time and place?"

"Let's go and ask my father, I think he is looking at the orientation panel right now!"

Off we went back through the shiny passages to the control room. Dref bent down and whispered something to his father who then turned around, looked at me and gave me an eerie smile. He then started keying something into a keyboard which in turn showed up a whole bunch of hieroglyphic gobbledegook on the big television screen in front of him.

Dref studied it carefully and then turned to me and said, "Father tells me that we are going to make several passes over the target area and then we will stop briefly and deliver you back. The problem right now is picking up a strong enough energy pulse. At the moment, the locator keeps swinging across to a major city maybe a few miles from where you want to be!"

"Just get me there, Dref, I'll find my way back, don't worry about that, but I am a bit apprehensive about the way in which you'll deposit me back on the ground; what if I shrivel up on the way or end up in the wrong time and place like we did before? If you're not there with me what happens then, will I be stuck there forever?"

"If that's all you're worried about, no problem, I'll come down with you and then get teleported back up afterwards when you're happy!"

Another half an hour passed, and I could feel the momentum of the craft changing. Maybe this is it. “Is this it, Dref, are we here?”

“Almost. We need to get to the teleport bay now, and when we are ready you must do exactly as I say.”

I was nervous but excited, and in a way, I was going to miss Dref. We went through the sliding doors and Dref motioned for me to stand next to him in the middle of the bay under a shaft of bright light. Again, the momentum changed, and we appeared to be stationary. “If we can’t see out, how do we know we are in the right place?” I asked.

Dref simply said, “Trust me, my father is an expert!”

CHAPTER 11

30th July 1966

We crashed to the ground with a sickening thud, and momentarily the wind was knocked out of me. Dref was up and looking around straightaway. “Hey Andy, get up and have a look around. Where are we? Looks to me like a big city.”

I struggled to my feet, and as I did so I realised that we were on a tin roof of some sort. As I looked around it became obvious that we were on top of a very large stadium of some description. I scanned the skyline looking for landmarks, then it dawned on me. Hell, we were on top of Wembley Stadium! Dref was looking at me waiting for an answer. “So much for your father being an expert, Dref. We are nowhere near my home. We are in London, the capital city of the United Kingdom!”

“Well, that’s pretty cool, and what’s going on here? Is it a contest arena or something?”

At that moment, a deafening roar went up from 90,000 people, and as I looked down, I could see the two football teams emerging from their respective tunnels. I was trying to work out who the teams were; it was too late in the year for the cup final, maybe it was a qualifying match for the World Cup next year, but I couldn't work out why the match was being played at Wembley. Just then the loudspeakers crackled into life and announced:

"WELCOME TO WEMBLEY STADIUM AND THE 1966 WORLD CUP FINAL!"

"DREF!" I shouted at the top of my voice above the roar of the crowd. "Not only are we in the wrong place, but we are also in the wrong year! We've gone a year too far; this event is not meant to be happening until next year! What the hell are we going to do now?"

"Whoops," said Dref quite casually. "Nothing to worry about, I'll send a message back up to my people and they will soon sort this minor problem."

"You may think it's a minor problem, but I really don't. Apart from that, with you looking like a Christmas cracker and me looking like a tramp, if we get caught up here, they'll lock us up and throw away the key!"

“I’ve activated my beam beacon,” said Dref. “We’ll just have to wait now for them to find a suitable opportunity to pick us back up.”

“Well, lay down then, Dref, so we are not so conspicuous up here. We may as well watch the game, it’s just about to start.”

“What is this ‘game’ as you call it? Do they fight to the death and then get taken away to be recycled?”

“What?! I thought your people were ultra-civilised. That sounds barbaric to me. We stopped doing things like that hundreds of years ago!”

Dref looking rather hurt and bemused said, “There’s nothing wrong with that, it was used as a punishment on those who didn’t adhere to the strict recycling code. If they were found guilty, they were put in an arena to fight it out, and the losers were sent off in the trash capsules to be recycled in space!”

“Are you serious?”

“Yes of course I am,” replied Dref. “But it was all a waste of time in the end because the recycling rules came in too late, and the damage had already been done, and the pollution was too great. Like I was telling you earlier that's why we were forced to start looking for somewhere else to live. Your people should really learn now how to take proper care of your planet now before it's too late!"

Dref was starting to annoy me now. How dare he preach to me about how we should look after our planet when he was the one with nowhere to go! Anyway, the match was about to start, and it looks like England are playing West Germany, well that's a turn up for the books!

Suddenly, Dref became interested as England won the toss and Bobby Moore kicked off. "So, you were going to tell me what this game is all about?"

I started to explain to him the basics of a game of football, but he wasn't very impressed, and he just nodded his head and laid down next to me to watch the match and try and figure it out for himself. I couldn't believe that here I was watching the World Cup final with England in it as well, when only a few weeks ago back home we were wondering if we were going to qualify even! This was a bizarre experience, and how was I going to be able to keep it secret when I eventually got back to my own time and place?

England has won the toss and the game has started. Dref was looking more confused by the minute! The game is moving quite fast and West Germany are pushing hard. Oh no, West Germany has scored already and we're only twelve minutes into the game. Dref was actually looking like he was starting to get interested. Another five minutes has passed, and it looks like Geoff Hurst is going to score, there's nobody close to challenge him, YES! It's in the back of the net. I leapt to my feet with excitement and together with the other 90,000 people giving out a deafening cheer, I swear Dref jumped so much I thought he was going to fall off the roof. Everything settled down again. Play had resumed and after a couple of minutes a nosey pigeon landed on the roof a few feet away from Dref.

The crowd settled down and play started again, England now taking the play to the West Germans. Meanwhile, the nosey pigeon is looking at Dref inquisitively, with its head cocked to one side, then started flapping its wings and fluttering in front of him. Next thing I knew, Dref starts shrinking in front of me and formalizing into a pigeon, which seemed to startle it and it took off and flew down towards the pitch, seconds later, Dref as a fully formed pigeon takes off after it. They are then chasing each other around the stadium, then up onto the opposite roof creating an amazing aerial display that was in fact distracting me from the match. But not for long, things were hotting up again, it was still 1-1 and fast approaching half time. The ref blew his whistle, and the teams went off the pitch back down the tunnel to the changing rooms for a short break.

With the game stopped, I cast my attention back to Dref and his pigeon friend, who both were still giving an aerobatic display, Dref showing off as usual. It was easy to tell which one was him, then they both did a steep dive and then landed right on the centre spot on the pitch. Maybe Dref was thinking he'd fancy a go at football, but luckily there were no players left on the pitch for him to formalize into, or that would have caused major problems. Suddenly, they both took off again and headed in my direction, one landing next to me, which I guessed was Dref and the other then turned and flew off into the distance. Almost immediately Dref started to turn back into human form again.

"Hey, Andy, that was fun! I haven't enjoyed myself so much since we were on those remote islands - what was it you called them, the Scillies? Sounds like a really weird name to me. Anyway, I'm getting a lot of strange signals from my beam beacon. I think it's because there are a lot of odd craft in the sky but none of them are mine."

"Well, that would be because we are close to the flight path for London Heathrow airport and if your people get mixed up with that lot when trying to retrieve us it will cause very big problems!"

"That's not going to happen," said Dref. "Our detection systems are extremely sensitive, and they will look for a pattern until they see a window of opportunity, and one of my signals is xy#~ positive, so they must be somewhere close."

As he said that, I was hearing the same strange noise I heard the morning I first met Dref. My thoughts were racing. Heck, if they showed up now all hell would break loose! On the other hand, did I want them to show up yet? It was only half time, and I wouldn't know the outcome of the match if we left now. I was looking up at the clear blue sky; I could see some passenger jets in the distance getting ready to land at Heathrow, but no sign of the mothership. But my thoughts about staying to the end of the match were soon to be ended.

"Andy, grab hold of me now!"

"What, why...?"

"NOW!"

There was a great WHOOSH like when you jump in the deep end off the high board at the swimming pool, then nothing for a few seconds as everything went black, and then with a thud we landed on the floor of the entry chamber in the mothership. Dref's brother was standing there waiting for us. He helped us up as we were a bit dazed and ushered us into what looked like a reception area, which was something I hadn't seen last time I was aboard.

Finally, Dref got around to introducing us: "Andy, this is my brother Mas, Mas this is Andy, my Earth friend."

Mas was slightly taller than Dref, but with almost identical features. He had a stern look about him and seemed much more business-like. Obviously, all the Mondernians, at least in Dref's family anyway, possessed the ability to speak in multiple languages. I wondered if they could all formalize the same as Dref or if that was something peculiar to him, that would be interesting! I asked Mas how come they were able to position the craft in such a way that it didn't cause a catastrophe with our own craft flying in and out of the airport?

Mas looked at Dref who nodded, seemingly they were telepathic as well, and he walked over to a console in the corner and to my astonishment the complete wall turned into a viewing area, and we were actually in space, and I was looking down on our beautiful blue planet Earth.

“That’s why!” exclaimed Dref. “They only brought our craft down into the stratosphere not into the atmosphere. With my beam beacon fully charged they were able to easily locate where we were and as soon as they locked on and I acknowledged, we were powered back up here. Now we’ve come further out to avoid any unnecessary detection while we programme the next exercise to get you back to yours, which shouldn’t be a problem, you weren’t far off after all!”

My brain was trying to take all this in, but one thought kept coming back to me: did we win the World Cup? I was going to have to wait another year to find out.

CHAPTER 12

Dref gave me one of their foil overalls to put on. “Here, put this on Andy, as it’s your second time up here now you need to be protected from radiation! We are going to orbit your pretty blue planet a few times and then we’ll turn on the time locator and see if we can put you down in the right place this time,” he said, laughing and giving me his silly grin. “But before you depart, my father would like to have a chat with you.”

Well, thinks me, I wonder what that is all about?

I still couldn’t really believe this was happening; maybe I was really dreaming. I pinched myself as hard as I could until the skin stung. No, this was real! I remember seeing the craft in the sky on that very first morning and thinking it looked like a cruise ship in the sky. I had only seen the equivalent of four rooms since I had been aboard, and I was inquisitive as to what was in the rest of the craft.

“Hey, Dref, you said you were going to give me a tour of your craft. C’mon then, show me around before I leave, I want to see what the rest of it is like. I may never have another chance.”

"Oh yes you will, trust me, we have big plans for you in the future, we could be seeing a lot of each other."

Ah, maybe that's what his dad wants to talk to me about.

So, off we went on a tour of the mothership, and I was absolutely stunned - it was a cross between a cruise ship and an aircraft carrier. At one point we were in what looked like an enormous aircraft hangar and docked inside were lots of smaller craft not much bigger than the average family car.
"Hey Dref, these are cool, what are these for then?"

"Don't touch them, Andy, they are all alarmed! They're our defender units, if we come under attack from unidentified or hostile craft, they are automatically deployed to seek and destroy."

"So, who drives them then?"

"We all do!" said Dref, as if I should have known.

"How can you do that when you're all operating the mothership?"

"No, Andy, I don't mean we actually get in and physically drive them, they are remote. They self-launch in the event of danger and we operate them from the central control area that you saw up top. My brothers mainly operate them; Mas especially is an ace, he can operate six at a time, and he's never lost one yet. But Tarie my other brother, he's still learning, and can only manage to operate two at a time. And me, well they will only let me control one at the moment, but I'm getting better. Soon I'll get a second one!"

"So, tell me, Dref, how often do you have to deploy these defender units?"

"Never in your galaxy, but in your neighbouring galaxies many times. There are a lot of parallel universes out there similar to yours and mine, but unlike ours they are not peaceful. They are very aggressive and are intent only on universal domination, but fortunately their aggression is not matched by what you would call common sense. Their lifeforms are cheap and have no meaning or fulfilment; live or die it makes no difference to them. Most of them have all but destroyed their planet homes, so because of their inferior mindset, our defender units with us in control, have always managed to outsmart them. Up until now that is!"

"I understand what you mean, Dref, about looking after the planet before it's too late. When I walk along the beach at home there is all sorts of stuff washed up on the shoreline and I often wonder what a danger it must be to the marine and wildlife that may find themselves tangled up in the plastic stuff, or even eating it. Then I look across the water at the massive oil refinery and the tall flames shooting out of the chimneys burning off the excess oil, and the stink from it if the wind is in the wrong direction makes you feel sick. That must be one bad ass lot of pollution going into the atmosphere, I should think. Then every so often there's a spillage from one of the big oil tankers and lumps of thick black tar end up getting washed up on the beach. YUK!"

"That's exactly the sort of thing that I was talking about," said Dref, "and it only gets worse and worse. It's happened in so many galaxies and that's why there are a lot of displaced beings out there in deep space now, all looking for new planets to colonise. I guarantee you that they won't have learnt their lesson and when they do find new planets on which to settle, they'll do the same thing all over again. The trouble is they think they are so clever, yet they are unable to recognise their own stupidity!"

What Dref was saying made a lot of sense and it started me thinking about the local tip, which the posh folk call a landfill site, but really it's just a great big hole in the ground which was left from old gravel pit workings, and literally everything gets tipped in there; the bin lorries tip their domestic waste in there, the farmers tip their farm waste in there, I've even seen an oil tanker tipping waste oil in there. But worst of all, there's a lane that runs down the side of one of the tip sites and it's in a bit of a dip so the road is lower than the built up ground next to it, and you can see horrible black gooey liquid oozing out of the side of the made-up ground leading up to the surface of the tip site. That really must be polluting the ground and water courses, yet nobody takes any notice of that; they just accept it. I can see exactly what Dref is talking about now. I thought he was exaggerating at first, but really, here it is, starting to happen already, right on my own doorstep!

"Hey, Andy, we're on the second orbit already. Look at your beautiful blue planet down there. There are very few like that left in neighbouring universes anymore. There were lots once upon a time, so the Elders tell me, but over time most of them have either been in collision with other space masses and dried out like that one there or there."

Dref was pointing at the moon and also Mars, I think.

“But the biggest problem, as I said earlier, has been the lifeforms destroying their own planets with pollution,” Dref reiterated yet again.

He was definitely trying to impress upon me the dangers that planet Earth will be facing in the future if we don’t change our ways. I was finding it hard to get my head around the fact that there were other planets out there resembling Earth.

Suddenly, Dref started waving frantically to beckon me over to the observation window. “Look over there, Andy. You see that weird machine that we are about to overtake? It looks like an ancient communications pod.”

As we got closer, I could just make out the shape; it was definitely a sputnik, maybe it was the Telstar that was launched into space about three years ago. “That’s not ancient, Dref, that’s one of our new communication satellites that was sent into space a few years ago.” Dref was about to make a comment, probably to the effect of how behind we are in technology, but I gave him one of my knowing looks and he thought better of it!

“Ok Andy, we need to get back down to the transport chamber. We’re about to enter the final run in on the last orbit to get in position to drop you.”

“Not just me, I hope. You’re coming as well, aren’t you? If it goes wrong again, I don’t want to be stranded in the wrong time and place forever!”

“‘Yes, of course, I’ll come as well, but I’m sure there won’t be a problem this time,” Dref replied confidently.

So, there we were back in the transport chamber and Dref’s brother Mas was there waiting for us. I still couldn’t get my head around how Dref’s family all looked the same as each other, just older versions. Mas wasn’t very communicative; I think he viewed me with suspicion. After all I must in effect be an alien as far as he was concerned. What a bizarre thought!

“Right,” said Dref. “Stand here next to me again, hands down by your side and stay perfectly still. Okay, Mas, we’re good to go.”

Although this was the fourth time I had been through this process, I was still very nervous, especially after the failure of the last attempt. Although that was a crazy experience ending up at Wembley Stadium watching a world cup final that hasn’t happened yet! But on the other hand, I could maybe even end up on the Moon or Mars! Mas gave Dref the nod and I braced myself. Here we go, the big whoosh, then everything is black.

CHAPTER 13

Wallop! With another sickening thud, we hit ground. I was disorientated, and for a few seconds I wondered why I couldn't move, I seemed to be pinned to the ground! As I cautiously opened my eyes I realised why; Dref had landed right on top of me!

"Get off me you big whelp. I can't move and can hardly breathe."

"No need to talk to me like that, at least you're home in one piece," retorted Dref in his once again cocky manner.

I sat up and looked around. Wow, he was right, we were actually back in Verdons Meadow, right at the spot where Dref had appeared in front of me as a giant lizard formalizing into a humanoid! All I had to do now was figure out the day, the time, and a plausible story as to where I had been for however long I had been away! We both stood up and looked around, still a little stunned and thinking about what to do next. We still had our silver suits on, so they had to come off for starters. I had my filthy scruffy clothes on underneath. "Dref, you need to take your suit off. What have you got on underneath?"

"My day suit of course!" Dref replied indignantly.

As he started to take it off, I could see immediately that what he meant by 'day suit' we would normally call 'birthday suit'; in other words, he was stark naked underneath!
"No, that's okay, Dref, leave it on for now. We'll sort something else out for you, just let me think for a minute."

"Right, I think firstly you need to decide whether you are going straight back to the mothership or if you're going to stay around for a bit and go back later. For me, it would be easier if you stayed for a while, that would at least help when I make excuses for where I've been these past few days, or however long we've been away. If I remember correctly, we told my Mum and Dad that you had come in on your parents' boat down on the river. Maybe I could work out an explanation around that idea? Anyway, what do you want to do, Dref, have you decided?"

"Well, Andy, we've been on a bit of a journey together, it might be fun to hang around for a while and watch the action when you go home!" said Dref sarcastically but with a devilish smile.
"I'll message my father and check that it's alright with them to transport me back later. I've got a full charge on my belt, so I should be safe to stay for a while. Is that okay?"

"That's a deal. Message your dad then while I try and sneak back home without being seen and fetch a change of clothes for both of us like I did before. Meanwhile, try and stay out of sight in that clump of bushes over there."

Wow! As I'm walking back across the meadow towards the house, have I got a sense of déjà vu or what? It wasn't helped by the fact that I didn't know what time of day it was or even the day of the week. But looking at the sun going down I guessed it was early evening. I was praying that Mum and Dad would be at the bottom of the garden away from the house picking fruit as they often did in the summer evenings, and that the girls were out at the recreation ground checking out the boys, which was their usual pastime!

I carefully approached the house and snuck into the field next door. There was a thick hedge separating it from our place and I figured that if I ran down the hedge line there were a few good vantage points where I could check out who was where and doing what!

As I thought, Mum and Dad were fruit picking next to the apple orchard. But also, there was a tent up in the field the other side of the orchard; it looked like the girls were getting ready to sleep out there for the night and I could see several of them buzzing around. What a stroke of luck! I ran back down the field, out of the gate and up our garden path to the front door. Hopefully the key was still under the plant pot.

Yes, it was! I quietly turned the key and pushed the door open and listened. I couldn't hear a sound, so I ran upstairs to my room, stripped off my disgusting clothes and stuffed them under my bed. It was then that I realised that I smelled worse than a skunk! Too bad, I didn't have time to wash now. I yanked the drawers open and quickly pulled on shorts and a shirt and grabbed a pair of my jeans and a t-shirt for Dref.

I was about to run down the stairs and make my escape before anyone saw me, but as I went past the bathroom, the door suddenly flung open and standing in front me was Michelle, one of the French girls. I don't know who was more shocked, her or me! Probably me, as I was trying to appear as if I wasn't really there but at the same time nearly fell down the stairs!

"Bonjour, Andy, where 'ave you bin? We did not know where you were?" she said hurriedly in her sexy French accent.

Much as I really fancied Michelle and I think she did me, I couldn't afford to get drawn into a conversation for obvious reasons. I put my finger to my lips: "Shhh, we had a problem with the boat - I'll tell you all about it later. Also, my friend Dref fell in the sea and has run out of dry clothes so I'm going to lend him some of mine," I said, pointing to the bundle that I was carrying. "Don't tell anyone you've seen me, I'll be back again soon, and I want to surprise everyone!" With that, I gave her a peck on the cheek and charged off down the stairs before she could question me further. If she did say anything, I would deal with that when I came back. But right now, I was worried about Dref and what he might be getting up to!

I ran across the road and back down the lane towards the paddock. Having got back there in double quick time, I looked behind the clump of bushes - no Dref! On top of that, the horses in the next field that belonged to Stef West, the chip shop owner's daughter, were going absolutely ballistic, charging round the field chasing each other, bucking and nipping at each other's backsides. I looked around and couldn't see Dref anywhere. I was just thinking, oh well, maybe he has gone back up to the mothership after all because he was fed up with waiting. The nags next door were coming around the field again on another charge, when one of them came galloping straight towards the fence where I was stood. I honestly thought it was going to leap straight over the top and land on me, when it dug its front hooves in the ground and came skidding to a halt right by the fence. Just as I began to relax it reared up on its hind legs and I thought, this is it, I'm going to get crushed or kicked in the face!

As the horse came back down onto all fours, it seemed to be getting smaller, and its features were changing; of course, it was Dref!

"Hey, Andy, what took you so long? I was getting bored, and these creatures next door were having great fun so I thought I would join them. I don't think they like me much though; they kept chasing me and biting my rear end."

I enlightened Dref that that was a sign of affection, especially as he was a stallion, which I had to explain was a male horse, and the truth was that they probably fancied him! But that was lost on Dref and I don't think he found that amusing! As he finished formalizing back into human form, the mares in the field all charged at the fence as he was trying to climb over it, and one of them nudged his backside as he was perched on the top, and sent him flying into the bushes. The group of horses snorted and neighed their approval and wandered off. I could no longer contain myself and burst out laughing. I threw him the clothes that I'd picked up from home and said, "Here, put these on and put your silver suit right under the bush there so that you can come back for it when you're ready to go."

Unfortunately, Dref had landed in a thorn bush and was more interested in plucking the thorns out of his backside than getting changed straightaway. “That was a very unfriendly thing to do seeing as I had just been playing with the long-legged creatures!” exclaimed Dref rather indignantly.

Eventually, he regained his composure and looking quite natural in my clothes, we set off for home.

“So, who is at your home, are the girl humans still there?” enquired Dref casually.

“Yes, they are, and it looks like they are camping in the orchard tonight. But I did bump into Michelle in the house, and I had to tell her that we had been away on your boat, and unfortunately had a problem. On top of that, you fell in the sea, and I had come to get you dry clothes!”

“I wouldn’t do such a stupid thing,” replied Dref. “I would become a fish!”

“Well, I know that, and you know that, but they mustn’t know that for obvious reasons, and I had to tell her something. As it is, we are still going to have a lot of explaining to do to my parents."

As we were walking past Allman's greenhouses, his vicious black dog came bounding up to us with the hair standing up on his back, growling and baring his teeth to us. I had already had one bad encounter with that deranged dog a few months back. I had stood my ground, but he launched himself straight at my throat. The reflex action of a swift foot into his underside soon sent him off yelping with his tail between his legs!

But this time was different, he must have remembered me and looked like he was going straight for the kill! I turned to warn Dref, and for a second, I didn't see him, I looked down and he had already formalized into dog mode, identical to old man Allman's dog and equally as vicious! Dref flew at the black beast and within seconds they were both rolling across the ground having a full-on scrap. I shouted at Dref just as one of them let out a loud yelp and Allman's dog scuttled off across the yard. Meanwhile, old man Allman came out to see what all the noise was about.

"You need to keep that dog of yours under control. If I see him around here again attacking mine, I'll shoot him!" bellowed the old man.

I was praying that Dref didn't change back whilst old Allman was there, otherwise that would cause mega problems, or he'd have a heart attack!

"Dref, stay there, don't change yet," I said as quietly as I could. It wasn't worth arguing with the old chap; I just turned and walked off down the lane, and once we were out of sight, I said to Dref, "It's okay now you can be human form again." I stopped for a few seconds while Dref returned to his full height.

"Hey, that was fun!" exclaimed Dref. "I think I saved you there, Andy. That beast was a bit bossy, but I managed to bite his ear and he didn't like that very much, that's why he surrendered!"

"Yes, you did do me a favour there, thanks. But please don't pull that formalizing stunt when you see my dog, Bruce, in a minute or that will completely blow your cover."

As we walked up the garden path from the front gate, we could hear the girls giggling just as they appeared around the corner of the house. "Hi guys, where have you been, we wondered where you were?" shrieked Natalie.

Michelle looked at me and winked, as if to say, I kept the secret!

Before Dref could say anything, I volunteered that we had a problem with the boat and got stuck out in the channel, which seemed to satisfy their curiosity.

“We’re all off down to the rec.,” said Michelle. “Why don’t you two come with us?”

“Maybe later, but for now we’ve got to go and make peace with my parents!”

CHAPTER 14

"Hey Andy, why couldn't we have gone with the girls and come back later to see your Elders?" asked Dref glumly.

"The thing is, Dref, that's not how it works here on planet Earth. We need to square things off with the Elders as you call them, seeing as we just disappeared for days on end. Once we've done that, then we can carry on and have some fun."

That seemed to cheer Dref up. I was starting to realise that maybe his kind didn't have the same sort of emotional attachments that we have, they seem to be much more clinical. Having said that, I do get the impression, that given the chance, Dref would form an emotional attachment with every girl he comes into contact with. We are certainly very similar in that respect.

As we made our way down the path towards the far end of our long garden where all the fruit and vegetables were grown, my Dad looked up and spotted us. He nudged my Mum who immediately stopped what she was doing and stood up straight with her hands on her hips. Oh hell, I thought, this was her war stance, which meant that we were in for a real bad tongue

lashing! "Dref, don't say anything to start with, let me do the talking."
"And where have you been?" was Mother's opening greeting!

"Oh, hi Mum, nice to see you too!"

"Don't you come that cocky attitude with me my boy. Explain yourself now!"

For one embarrassing moment I thought she was going to take a swipe at me, but she glanced at Dref, who she still hadn't acknowledged, and thought better of it, I think. I loved her really, but that was her ultimate humiliation tactic, whacking me around the ear in front of my friends when she thought I'd overstepped the mark!

"Well, we went out in Dref's Mum and Dad's boat, and sailed out past The Point into the main channel. We were about ten miles out past the island, and the boom snapped. We tried to motor back in, but then ran out of petrol; the current caught us and took us out even further and we spent a couple of days and nights drifting before a passing fishing boat took us in tow and bought us back in to the river."

I realised immediately Mother was about to turn her attention to Dref and that he was about to get a verbal roasting from her as well, when Dad stepped in. “And next time you use some of my gear and blow it to pieces, like the battery charger for example, at least have the good manners to come and tell me. Don’t just go off and enjoy yourself. Apart from that, you didn’t even tell us where you were going, and we didn’t even know that you had gone.”

I felt bad about that for a number of reasons; my Dad was normally a placid guy who would help anyone with anything, and his tool shed, and workshop was pristine, everything had its proper place. Out of the corner of my eye I could see Dref fidgeting uneasily. Clearly, he was feeling uncomfortable and was sensing the tension. I had to somehow bring this to a close so that we could move on. Dref was starting to focus on a blackbird that was busily extracting a fat juicy worm from the freshly dug vegetable patch, and I thought to myself, any moment now he’s going join that blackbird, and both my parents will probably die of shock on the spot!

So that was it, I was going to have to apologise profusely, promise never to do anything so stupid again and generally grovel and swear that I would make it up to them.

Again, my Dad came to the rescue. “Okay, okay, we get the message. You start by making yourselves useful and carry these baskets of fruit down and putting them in the kitchen, and while you’re there, you can put the kettle on.”

Mother just scowled at Dad and then us, and I knew she was thinking we were getting off too lightly, but she rarely went against Dad. Quickly, before anyone changed their minds, we gathered up the baskets and made our way back down to the house.

We put the fruit baskets in the kitchen, and I put the kettle on as Dad had asked. I turned around to switch it on and Dref was already filling his face with strawberries and raspberries. “Hey, don’t eat it all, or we’ll be in even more trouble, are you hungry or what?”

Dref looked at me, surprised, “Hungry? I’m starving! It seems like we haven’t eaten properly for days. Apart from which, this food is similar to what we used to grow many years ago on Mondern, before the powerful and careless ones who were supposed to look after our planet, allowed the pollution to get so bad that the entire eco system collapsed and nothing would grow anymore, so that eventually it would no longer sustain life, and as you now know, those who didn’t perish were forced to leave the planet and seek out other worlds on which we may be able to survive. Having said that, Andy, your planet Earth I think suits me fine. That's why I wanted to take the opportunity of coming back with you for a while longer. I just need to persuade my family about the benefits of settling here. Maybe they could come for a visit, that would do it, I'm sure!"

Oh heck, I thought. Life is about to get very complicated again! I was eager to divert Dref's train of thought, to try and stop him going down a route that I was not really ready to contemplate, at least not yet anyway. "Hey Dref, why don't we go down to the park where the girls have gone? They'll be expecting us, and it should be a bit of a laugh. Besides, they were pleased to see you anyway when we got back earlier. I'll go and tell my parents we're going out."

Before Dref could answer, I ran down the garden to the apple orchard to find them and let them know what we were planning to do.

"Hey Mum, hey Dad, we're just going down the park for a while to meet up with the girls and some other friends. We won't be long."

"You make sure you're not, and don't go disappearing again without telling us. I don't trust that Derf friend of yours, or whatever his name is. You haven't been quite yourself since he turned up, so go careful, do you hear me?"

"Yes Dad, loud and clear, and his name is Dref not Derf!"

"Whatever, it sounds like the name of a washing powder! Be off with you, and don't be late or there'll be big trouble when you get back."

When I got back down to the kitchen, I found Dref sat on the floor by the dog's bed with Jinx the cat on his lap and the dog's head resting on his knee.

"Wow, that's a sight for sore eyes, I'm surprised you're not chasing each other around the garden!"

"I was tempted, but as they are two different species, I couldn't decide which one to formalize to, but I would have done if you'd have been much longer." Dref said with a glint in his eye, knowing that seeing an extra dog or cat running around the garden would have most likely given me another headache with my parents, who for now at least had got over their initial rant at us having disappeared for several days.

"C'mon then, Dref, let's get on down to the park if that's what you want to do, and we can chat on the way."

"How far away is it?" asked Dref.

"It's only about ten minutes' walk, but while we're walking, you can tell me a bit more about your planet Mondern and what really happened and how you think you're going to arrange for your family to land on my planet Earth just to see if they like it here. I don't really know how you've managed to stay undetected so far, but even so, if the authorities had even the slightest suspicion that you and your folks were here, in other words, if they suspect that there's an unidentified flying object buzzing around they will pull out all the stops to intercept it, and maybe shoot it down or even capture it and everyone in it and take you all prisoner. I've seen it happen before."

"Really!" said Dref in astonishment. "That must have been a primitive sub species from the Zong system, they have been enemies of ours for a millennium, but their technology is far inferior to ours. They never developed the necessary screens and shields to protect and disguise themselves as we have. They've always relied on their light speed to get them out of trouble. But obviously it didn't work when they came into your orbit, unless of course they had a malfunction. Ha! You wait 'til I tell my folks; they will be most interested to learn of the Zongists' fate!"

"So, now that you know what happened to the Zong people, how can you be sure that you can get your folks down here safely without the same thing happening to them?"

"I don't know yet, Andy, well, not completely anyway, I'm still working on it, but it'll come to me. C'mon let's go and see the lovely girl creatures!"

When we arrived at the park, surprise, surprise, they were nowhere to be seen.

"Looks like we missed them, Dref, bad luck. I tell you what, let's climb to the top of that big fir tree by the gate over there. You can see the whole of the park from the top of there; they may be hiding behind the changing rooms next to the tennis courts. But no formalizing and chasing birds or dogs, or anything else for that matter. If anyone sees you doing that they'll freak out and that would be the end of your Earth visit. Just save that trick for emergency only."

We started to shin up the tree, me one side and Dref the other. Once he got the hang of it, he raced ahead of me up to the top like a monkey. The branches were spread out at the top which was handy really because we were both able to perch there side by side. From down below we must have looked like a couple of big crows sat on a nest! We looked all around but couldn't see a soul, then suddenly I spotted them running along the other side of the hedge line. I couldn't believe it! We must have beaten them there; I guess they must have walked the long way around and come through the old gravel pit and then cut across the churchyard.

"There they are, Dref. Look, over there. They will be heading through the gate here in a couple of minutes, and they won't have a clue that we're up here. Let's surprise them, shall we?"

"Yes, why not," replied Dref. "As they walk through the gate, I could hang upside down and make noises of a tree creature, that would surprise them!"

With that, the first of the three girls came through the gate and Dref swung into action, hanging off the branch upside down. He was swinging like a monkey, then came a sharp crack and the branch he was hanging on started to give. I shouted, "Dref, look out, grab my hand!" But it was too late. There was a second crack and Dref and the branch crashed to the ground and missed Natalie by inches. She screamed and the other girls ran to her and all three knelt down by Dref who was not moving and looked like he was either unconscious or dead! I slid down the trunk of the tree scraping my hands and knees in the process, amidst a thousand thoughts flashing through my mind in those few seconds it took me to get down - first and foremost: What will happen when the hospital discovers he's an alien?!

On ground level, the girls were becoming hysterical, so I had to take control. Dref's wrist was clearly broken, as his arm was outstretched, his hand looked to be several inches away from his arm and connected only by skin. Clearly, he was still breathing, so that was a good sign, and there didn't appear to be any blood anywhere, another good sign. "Okay, Natalie, go over the road to old Mrs. Johns' house, knock on the door and tell her that our friend has had a mishap and ask her if she can give you an ice pack out of the fridge. You other two girls, stop sniffling and go over and sit on that bench while I try and sort Dref out. I may need you to go to the phone box up on the corner to call an ambulance. Just give me a couple of minutes!"

I carefully moved the broken branch away from Dref and made sure he was still breathing alright. His eyelids started fluttering and it looked like he was beginning to come around. "Dref, can you hear me, are you alright?" With that, he sat bolt upright and looked as if he was about to get up and run off! "Hey, take it easy, you've just fallen out of the tree. I think you've broken your wrist, look at it!" Without saying a word, Dref looked down at his hand which was literally hanging off his wrist, he grabbed it with the other hand, gave it a twist and a shove and pushed it back into place. He then held it up wriggled it about and it appeared to be absolutely fine again, but it made me feel quite sick watching him, especially as to start with it looked like his hand was about to drop off!

"Dref, how did you do that? I thought we were going to have to take you to hospital to get it mended."

"Mondernians are physically very different to humanoids. We self-heal, in the same way that we can formalize into other creatures in our vicinity. In fact, if you had not told me not to, I may well have formalized into a bird like that one just over there and flown to the ground rather than falling like a bag of garbage!"

"Well, at least you are okay, that's the main thing. Look, Natalie is just coming back with a bag of ice and the other two have just realised you're okay and are coming over to see you."

The girls crowded around Dref and hugged him like he was a long-lost hero! He lapped it up, loved every minute of it.

Natalie carefully placed the ice pack on his wrist which was already better, causing her some confusion, but she let it pass. I think he thought it was a very worthwhile fall!

"Let's go over to the clubhouse, and I'll buy us all a coke. I've got some change in my pocket."

Amy and the other two girls liked that idea and helped Dref up, which of course he loved and played on it a bit, so off we went to the clubhouse.

CHAPTER 15

Sunny, the bar steward, was in the clubhouse as usual tending to the bar, and really everything else to do with the club; I swear he actually sleeps in the cellar sometimes! He's a bit of a strange character really but doesn't have an unkind word to say about anyone.

"What are you lot doing in here so early?" boomed Sunny from under the bar where he was emptying the drip trays. "I suppose you want five glasses and two drinks as usual!"

"No, it's ok, Sunny. Drinks are on me today; we'll have five glasses of coke please. There's been a bit of a mishap, my friend Dref here fell out of the tree by the gate, and the girls are in shock."

"Well, in that case, are you sure you don't want something a little stronger?" asked Sunny.

That caused a giggle from the girls, who replied in unison, "Yes, please."

"You can't have anything stronger, you're all too young!" said Sunny, roaring with laughter at his own joke, which was a wind up. Hence the name Sunny - he was always laughing at his own jokes - but the girls were not amused.

Dref, meanwhile, was paying a lot of attention to the fruit machine, which was randomly flashing, as they do. When I walked over to it, I could see why … the scene on the front that was flashing was one of stars, spaceships and alien creatures. I chuckled to myself and thought, this'll be interesting!

"Hey, Andy, what is this ancient machine? An early transponder?"

Before I could reply, Sunny shouted from the other side of the bar. "Tell your friend not to be so cheeky! That's our brand-new fruit machine, it was only delivered yesterday, and come and get these drinks before I tip them away."

The girls went to the bar for the drinks and sat down at a table while I went over to Dref to explain to him what the fruit machine was for. He was a bit confused at first, because obviously they didn't have anything like that on Mondern. So, I thought the easiest thing was to put a coin in the slot, which gave us ten plays and show him how it worked rather than tell him. So, I put the coin in and pulled the handle. As the reels spun round, lights started flashing randomly and chasing themselves around the console as they do, lighting up the different pay-outs that can, but rarely, be won. Dref looked startled for a minute, but as the reels stopped spinning, first one, then two, then three cherries appeared, an electronic bell in the machine rang out signalling a win, and five coins dropped into the tray.

“That’s beginners’ luck!” shouted Sunny from the bar. “I bet you couldn’t do that again.”

I pulled it again, and sure enough, nothing. I used up the remaining credits and started to put the winnings in, having put the original coin back in my pocket. Dref, meanwhile, who had been staring inventively at the machine, nudged me to one side and said, “My turn!”

“Go on then, see if you can do any better than me.” He grabbed the handle and pulled, but he didn’t let go of it straightaway, he kept hold of it and let it go back gradually, whilst all the time concentrating on the reels. As each reel stopped, he stopped the handle briefly until the next reel stopped then repeated the process until they were all stopped. Instantly, the bells started ringing and ten pounds worth of shiny coins dropped into the tray. The girls came running over to see what was going on; all of a sudden, Dref was their new best friend!!

“Wow, looks like you’ve got the magic touch!” exclaimed Natalie. Dref just shrugged it off and put another coin in, again, letting the handle back slowly. This time he hit the jackpot! Fifty pounds flashed up and the coins just kept coming, spilling all over the floor. Meanwhile, Sunny looked like he was about to blow a fuse.

“Okay, that’s enough you lot, pick up your winnings, finish your drinks and go. Either the machine isn’t set up right or you’re fiddling it somehow. It’s not normal for it to pay out like that. Anyway, you’re not even supposed to be playing it under the age of eighteen.”

“Aaww Sunny, c’mon, don’t spoil the fun!”

“I’ll give you don’t spoil the fun! Here, take this bag and put your winnings in and clear off before you get me the sack.”

With that, we scooped up all the coins and put them in the bag and made our way out into the field with Dref looking confused and disgruntled. We sat down on the grass and counted out the money, nearly sixty pounds in all. I suggested we divided it up equally between us, which pleased the girls, although I wondered what Dref was going to do with his share, unless he was planning on a long stay!

Amy had clearly taken a fancy to Dref, she was almost sat on his lap! “Hey Dref, how did you manage to win on the machine? Do you have a secret method that you can share with us or was it just luck?” she asked.

“That was easy,” replied Dref. “You control the speed of the reels by the way you let the handle back then you listen for the clicks and watch the reels slowing down, then set them where you want them, easy!”

We shared the coins out equally; when Dref said he didn’t want his and gave his share to the girls as well, instantly he became their new hero. We were just about to decide what to do next, when a massive German Shepherd dog came bounding up to us. He looked quite friendly to start with, sniffing all around us and wagging his tail. Until he came close to Dref! Immediately his hackles came up on his back and he started backing away, growling and baring his teeth. The girls suddenly grabbed hold of each other, afraid that he may turn on them. Dref just started staring the dog out. In my mind I was panicking at what was going to happen next, I thought that faced with danger, Dref may formalize into a dog as well and they would have an all-out scrap. That would be the worst nightmare ever and the girls would freak out big time! The dog started barking and snarling. Dref looked at me and gave a nod of his head. He stood up and started running down towards the trees by the side of the river. The dog was in hot pursuit, but Dref was running like the wind and outpacing the dog.

They disappeared behind the trees, and there was a ferocious snapping, barking and growling. I immediately thought: Oh my god, he's got Dref!

The girls started screaming hysterically. "Andy, do something, he'll rip Dref to pieces. That's old man Brown's dog over at the chicken farm and he's really vicious. Go on, do something!"

I grabbed one of the metal posts holding the rope up to keep people off the cricket pitch and ran down to where Dref and the dog had gone. The barking had now changed into a high-pitched yelping. As I ran to where they were behind the trees I could immediately see why. Dref had formalized into a dog once he was out of sight of the girls, to protect himself! Clever thinking. Just as I got there, I saw Brown's dog get tossed up in the air by Dref and he landed straight in the river, Dref jumped straight in after him, gave him a right old going over and then dragged the half-drowned animal out of the river by the scruff of the neck.

The dog spluttered and threw up a load of water, then shook himself and made off across the field with his tail between his legs!

Almost instantly, Dref started to change back into human form, which still freaked me out every time he did it.

“Hey Andy, that ugly hound doesn’t look so clever now does he?” said Dref, as he turned to watch the dog disappearing over the hill going back to where he came from.

“I ran as far away as I could so the girls couldn’t see what I was about to do, like you said. But I had no choice really, I did it to protect both you and the girls as the ugly one was getting far too aggressive and showing off.”

“I realise that Dref. You did well. Now let’s get back up to the girls or they will be in a panic thinking that we have both been eaten alive. Anyway, looking at those clouds up there, I think we are in for a storm.”

Dref looked at me quizzically, and I guessed that he didn’t understand what I meant by ‘storm’. So, I explained to him that a storm occurs when there is a change in the weather, and as I said it there was a loud clap of thunder which really startled Dref and he threw himself to the ground!

"Come on, Dref, up you get, it wasn't that bad. We had better run back to the girls. I expect they are frightened witless!"

As we were running, I explained to Dref that the noise was thunder, which is a soundwave caused by lightning occurring when positive and negative charges come together to cause a giant spark. To my surprise he appeared to understand that explanation completely!

As we ran across the top of the hill and the girls came into view, sure enough they were sat in a huddle, holding on to each other as if the world was about to end. As soon as they spotted us, they jumped up and ran towards us. They were trembling. and shaking, almost on the verge of hysteria. I don't know what panicked them most, the thought of Dref or me being torn to pieces by the mad dog, or the risk of being struck by lightning.

Amy spoke first between the sobs. "Crikey, we were so scared! From the horrible animal noises coming from down by the river, we thought you were both done for, then there was the great bolt of lightning that hit out in the next field. We thought we were all going to die!"

Dref looked a bit bemused at their emotion, and was about to say something, but I quickly tried to reassure them. "Okay, we didn't get torn to shreds, as you can see. We're fine and nobody has been struck by lightning, so let's get back up to the clubhouse quickly." If only they knew the truth: I was actually scared stiff of being stuck out in the open in a thunderstorm, ever since I was nearly struck by lightning one night a few years ago when I was out camping only a short distance from where we are now when I was with the scouts.

As we were walking back across the field, the strangest thing happened, we all started scratching our heads as it felt as if something was crawling in our hair and as we looked at each other, our hair had started to stand up on our heads, due to all the static in the atmosphere from the storm. Dref thought this to be really amusing, and in fact was acting a bit peculiar, almost as if his whole body was energised, instead of walking normally, he seemed to be almost prancing, a bit like a spring lamb, which the girls thought was really funny and started mimicking him.

The sky was getting darker by the minute and the wind was getting stronger, yet it was such a warm breeze. A few big drops of rain started falling, and within seconds it started pouring, followed by a massive simultaneous flash and bang, and then…nothing!

I came to first and sat up and looked around me. The rain was still thrashing down on us. I looked around and for a terrible moment I thought that the three girls were all dead, but gradually they started to sit up one by one, all shivering and frightened. Maisy spoke first. "Andy, what happened, where's Dref?" He was nowhere to be seen.

However, he was the least of my problems right now, apart from which he was big enough and able enough to look after himself. Right now, my priority was to calm down what were now three near hysterical girls and get them to safety before anything else happened. Clearly, a lightning bolt had struck very close to us and the force from it had stunned us all momentarily. But where was Dref?

"Come on, girls, jump up and let's run up to the clubhouse as quick as we can before the storm gets even worse."

Amy was definitely partly dazed and still in shock and having difficulty in putting one foot in front of the other. I put my arm under her and helped her along while the others ran on ahead.

As we were making our way back, I could hear a high-pitched buzzing sound. I thought I was imagining it at first, or perhaps it was the aftermath of the thunderbolt. Then I realised where I had heard that noise before.

Of course! It was that first morning when I met Dref, and I fell off my bike looking up and saw his mothership for the first time! So that's where Dref was; he had been transported back up when the thunder bolt had struck, and they must have harnessed the power from the lightning bolt maybe? Well, at least he is safe hopefully. I'll just have to tell the girls that he took fright and ran off back to the river to find his boat. I dare not tell them what really happened. I wonder if I'll ever see him again. Annoying as he was sometimes, I was getting quite used to having him around, and moreover we got involved in some of the hairiest adventures and did things that nobody would ever believe unless they were actually there with us.

We carried on running towards the clubhouse. The rain was now torrential, more like a monsoon, with a constant rumble of thunder and the occasional flash of lightning. The buzzing from the mothership was subsiding, but Amy was almost hysterical and seemed to be rivetted to the ground every time there was a clap of thunder. I ended up picking her up and carrying her and shouting at the other two to keep running and not to stop until they reached the clubhouse.

We crashed through the door of the clubhouse into the porch, to be confronted seconds later by Sunny bellowing, “What the hell’s going on out there?”

As soon as he saw the distressed state the girls were in, he softened his approach. “Look at the state of you all, you’ll catch your death of cold! Come in here in the warm, and I’ll get some towels out of the changing rooms.”

Gradually, the girls calmed down and by the time Sunny came back with the towels they had stopped sobbing but were still shaking like jellies on a washing machine! “Here, wrap these around you and dry yourselves off and I’ll go and make some hot chocolate for you all to warm you up from the inside!”

Good old Sunny, I thought, he is human after all.

My biggest problem right now was to be able to think up a plausible explanation as to where Dref had disappeared to, but at the same time without raising any suspicion as to who and what he really is! The best I could think of was to say that when the lightning bolt hit close by us and the girls were momentarily dazed, Dref was worried about his parents on the boat and was going to run back along the river path to make sure that both they and the boat were okay! It was of course a great big porky, but in the circumstances, and to protect Dref's true identity it had to be done!

Sunny brought over the mugs of hot chocolate, and we all sat on the old sofa in the corner and Sunny pulled up a stool and said, "Right, now tell me what all this is about?"

The girls all seemed to find their tongues at the same time, much to Sunny's annoyance, but gradually they all calmed down and with a little help from me, he got the general idea of what had happened. Basically, that we nearly got struck by lightning, we got soaking wet in the storm, and Dref had done a runner back to his boat.

"Well!" exclaimed Sunny. "I think you should all consider yourselves very fortunate that you've escaped in one piece, and I hope your other young friend got back to his boat safely. He was a nice enough lad, but there was something odd about him that I couldn't quite put my finger on!"

As the storm began to subside and a few breaks started to appear in the clouds, we decided it was time to walk home. The girls were quite subdued and had very little to say walking back up the lane.

“Do you think your friend Dref is alright?” asked Amy.

“I’m sure he’s fine, he just had to get back to his folks.” I replied confidently.

As we arrived at the end of the lane and the girls went their separate ways home, I had a sneaking feeling that I hadn’t seen the last of Dref.

Each time a trainer plane flew over on its way back to the old airfield I found myself wondering where Dref’s mothership was right now, and what their end game was going to be!

The next few weeks carried on much as normal, with parties on the beach and out in the fields behind Bluebell Woods, but for me anyway, things didn’t feel quite the same now that Dref had gone. In fact, I was finding everything a bit boring after the escapades that me and Dref had been on together! At night I would sleep in the tent in the garden and look up at the stars and imagine Dref’s mothership sailing through the sky and casting my mind back to the day that I had actually seen it and then came upon Dref in his giant lizard mode.

When I arrived back home from yet another fishless fishing trip down the river, my mother was eager to tell me that Amy had called round to the house.

“Is she your girlfriend?” Mother nosily asked.

“Of course not,” I replied. “We are just friends!”

I walked off down to my tent before Mother asked any more prying questions. I unzipped the flap and was about to jump on my sleeping bag but saw there was a note tucked under the corner of it. **‘Andy, meet me at Aylings meadow after tea tonight about sevenish. I must speak to you, it’s really important, it’s about Dref! Love Amy x’**

Look out for the next book in the series

"Dref – The Revelation"

If you would like to leave feedback
and follow Dref's journey blog
coming to Planet Earth,

log in to:-

www.aliendref.com

Enjoy the Journey!

Sam Bryhar